Tales from the Big House: Nostell Priory

To my daughter Lucy, with love

Other titles by Michael J. Rochford

Wakefield Then & Now: Extraordinary Tales from the Merrie City

Tales from the Big House: Nostell Priory

900 Years of its History and People

Michael J. Rochford

PEN & SWORD
HISTORY

First published in Great Britain in 2018 by
Pen & Sword History
an imprint of
Pen & Sword Books Ltd
47 Church Street
Barnsley
South Yorkshire
S70 2AS

ISBN 978 1 52670 270 8

Typeset in Ehrhardt by
Aura Technology and Software Services, India
Printed and bound in the UK by TJ International Ltd,
Padstow, Cornwall

Pen & Sword Books Limited incorporates the imprints of Atlas,
Archaeology, Aviation, Discovery, Family History, Fiction, History,
Maritime, Military, Military Classics, Politics, Select, Transport,
True Crime, Air World, Frontline Publishing, Leo Cooper,
Remember When, Seaforth Publishing, The Praetorian Press,
Wharncliffe Local History, Wharncliffe Transport,
Wharncliffe True Crime and White Owl.

For a complete list of Pen & Sword titles please contact
PEN & SWORD BOOKS LIMITED
47 Church Street, Barnsley, South Yorkshire S70 2AS, United Kingdom
E-mail: enquiries@pen-and-sword.co.uk
Website: www.pen-and-sword.co.uk

Contents

Picture credits

Nostell Priory, from *A Series of picturesque views of castles and country houses in Yorkshire, principally in the northern division of the West Riding, from sketches made by Mr. E. Healey*, published in 1885.

Preface

In this book I chart some of the astounding stories about the people who called Nostell Priory and its environs their home. Comprising a grand house, built in the eighteenth century, complete with stunning parklands, Nostell has been run as a popular tourist attraction since the early 1950s.

But the tales you're about to read here cover almost 1,000 years of history. We begin at the time of the foundation of the Priory of St Oswald – Nostell's priory – progressing to the turbulent time of the Dissolution of the Monasteries in the 1530s, when the priory, which by then had operated from the site for over four centuries, was closed down and sold to one of the greedy Crown officials who'd dissolved it. From there our journey continues ever onwards. First to the tenure of the Gargraves, who were Nostell's owners during the second half of the sixteenth century, and then to the Winns, who arrived in the 1650s and have never left. With episodes of poison, murder, elopement and financial ruin, these tales are full of mystery, intrigue, suspense, romance and excitement!

I have consulted many sources, including original documents principally held in The National Archives; the Borthwick Institute at the University of York; the West Yorkshire Archive Service in Wakefield; Lambeth Palace Library; the Special Collections at the University of Leeds; and Barnsley and Wakefield Local Studies libraries, along with countless antiquarian and modern books. A detailed description of these sources appears at the end of the book, allowing for easy identification of any of the documents cited, which will hopefully inspire further study.

Where I have transcribed detailed passages from these original documents, I have usually modernized the spellings for ease of reading, but when quoting shorter passages, the original spelling has been retained. I have also used dates in the Old Style, Julian calendar, where relevant, hence January 1585/6 and so on.

I must thank Dr Charles Kelham of Doncaster Archives for his help in translating a particularly tricky Latin indictment; assistance that has helped to disprove a long-held version of a particular story concerning one of the owners of Nostell during the reign of Queen Elizabeth I, which I shan't spoil here.

Thank you also to Sylvia Thomas of the Yorkshire Archaeological and Historical Society who kindly gave permission for the use of passages from *Reminiscences of Nostell*, an unpublished manuscript in the YAHS collections written by the Nostell family doctor, T.G. Wright, in 1887.

My appreciation also goes out to the staff at all the local studies libraries and record offices, and any other copyright holders who have granted permission for the reproduction of images from their collections, especially Wendy Jewitt of Wakefield Library.

Special thanks must go to Linne Matthews, a dedicated and skilful editor who always goes above and beyond the call of duty, and has my sympathy for having to read through all my (not always brief) email correspondence!

Finally, heartfelt gratitude to my beloved wife, Caroline, who has shown unflinching support throughout this project, and who listened with apparent interest as I read out passages of the text (over and over again), suggesting crucial amendments and historical insight, all done while carrying and then giving birth to our beautiful daughter Lucy. Caroline, you truly are my soulmate.

Michael J. Rochford
Wakefield, 2018

Nostell Priory from the lake, from *Old Yorkshire*, volume five, edited by William Smith.

The church of St Michael and Our Lady at Wragby.

Introduction

Foundation

O n 9 March 1544, the English lawyer Dr Thomas Legh devised by
will several properties including his 'howse called Sainte Oswalds
in Yorkshire', which he gave to his wife, Joan.

This 'howse' was in fact the recently dissolved Augustinian priory,
dedicated to the Northumbrian martyr king, St Oswald. It had been founded
in the early twelfth century during the reign of Henry I (1100–1135) on land
that formed part of the honour of Pontefract, now within the boundaries of
the parish of Wragby, some 6 miles south-east of the city of Wakefield, and
around the same distance south-west of Pontefract.

The site on which it stood is noted for possessing a large pool of water,
which the nineteenth-century historian and all-round know-it-all, the
Reverend Joseph Hunter, suggested, 'might even deserve to be called a
lake'. The sixteenth-century antiquary John Leland, visiting Nostell at some
point between the mid-1530s and the mid-1540s, described this as a 'praty
pole' (let's assume he meant pretty pool), which, he said, 'lyeth … at the
west ende of the house'. Today this body of water is known as Upper Lake
and Middle Lake, with the separate Lower Lake just to the north of the
present-day house.

An ancient Latin record speaks of *'apud veterum locum'*, that is to say,
the 'old place', an earlier monastic house on the estate, believed by some to
have been built on ground now occupied by the church of St Michael and
Our Lady, otherwise known as Wragby parish church. The latter edifice was
constructed by 1533, the former over 400 years earlier. The same ancient
record, found in the *Nostell Act Book*, contains an account of the foundation
of Nostell's priory and its monastic order, written during the late fourteenth
or early fifteenth century. This account, composed during the time of the
then prior Robert de Quixley, is known as *Gesta*, ('history' or 'events' in
English) owing to its longer Latin title, which, in full is: *De Gestis et Actibus*

The Reverend Joseph Hunter, FSA, the nineteenth-century topographer who wrote a detailed chapter on Nostell Priory in the second volume of his 1831 book *South Yorkshire: the History and Topography of the Deanery of Doncaster.*

Priorum Monasterique Sancti Oswaldi de Nostell A Prima Fundacione Usque Ad Dominum Robertrum Qwyxlay.

Robert de Quixley was Nostell's prior from 1393 to 1427, and a story from the priory's early days that had been passed down the generations still endured during his tenure, and has now entered the stuff of legend. The tale that follows has been told many times and opinion as to its veracity is divided, but it goes like this.

Accompanying Henry I as he travelled in the north, waging war against the troublesome Scots, was a man named Ralph Aldlave (sometimes Adlave, othertimes Aldave, but Radulpho Aldlavus in *Gesta*). He was described as King Henry's '*capellanus et co'fessor*', in other words, his royal chaplain and confessor. Unfortunately, poor Aldlave was taken sick while the royal party was at Pontefract Castle and it was decided he would stay behind while he recovered. One day, as his condition began to improve, he decided to pass the time hunting in the local woods, when suddenly, he was conveyed by the divine inspiration of the Holy Spirit to the land called Nostell: '*sita est et vocatur le Nostell'*. Here he came upon a group of pious hermits who lived in these woods, worshipping at their chapel of St Oswald: *'capella S'ci Oswaldi'*. Despite this dedication to St Oswald, the Northumbrian martyr king, Hunter described the settlers as 'the small community of hermits of St James'. On the same theme, the antiquary John Burton, who published *Monasticon Eboracense* in 1758, included in his footnotes a translation of a now 'lost document' dated to the final decade of the eleventh century that revealed a grant of a manor in Yorkshire to 'Gilbert, the hermit of St James de Nostel and to the brethren of the same house, and their successors, serving God there', evidently suggesting an earlier dedication. And to confuse matters further, Ordnance Survey issued a map of Yorkshire in 1892, marking the parish church as having being built 'on [the] site of St James' Monastery'. And the editors of volume three of *A History of the County of York*, published in 1974 (part of the Victoria County History series), had this to say about the place Aldlave found the hermits: 'on or near the site where the Augustinian priory was afterwards founded there was a hermitage dedicated in honour of St James in which a certain unknown number of hermits were congregated.'

So rapt was he by these men, the rejuvenated Aldlave resolved to join their group at once. With the consent of the king, Aldlave not only became part of the community, but also their master at a new monastery, which was comprised of Augustinian canons and enriched with vast endowments from eager benefactors.

The author of *Gesta* conveniently dated the story to 1121. This is the same year that Henry I granted the canons 12d per day from land he held in York. And the following year the king affirmed, by Royal Confirmation, significant donations that had been gifted to the priory by several notable patrons; these included mills, fisheries, bovates of land, meadows, and several churches and chapels in Yorkshire and beyond. However, it is recorded elsewhere that the hermits had made their transition to Augustine canons by 1120, making it clear that the order was already firmly established at the site by 1121.

The first prior at Nostell was called Adelulf and many historians, from John Burton onwards, have claimed that Adelulf and Ralph Aldlave were one and the same person. This appears to be a misleading conflation for the author of *Gesta* explained that Aldlave was buried at the 'old place', a reference to

An Augustinian Canon,
depicted in Reverend
Batty's *Historical Sketch of
the Priory of St Oswald's
Priory at Nostel*.

the fact that the canons had relocated to a new site closer to the pool (or fishpond) mentioned by Hunter, having received both papal and royal consent to do so. Prior Adelulf, meanwhile, was buried at Carlisle, where he was diocesan bishop from 1133.

John Leland repeated the story about Aldlave when he said of his own visit to Nostell: 'Where the paroche church of S. Oswaldes is now newly buildid' – an early name for the church of St Michael and Our Lady, built by 1533 – 'was in Henry the first tyme a house and a chirche of poore heremites, as in a woody cuntery, on tille one Radulphus Aldlaver, confessor to Henry the first, began the new monasterie of chanons, and was first prior of it himself.'

But did Ralph Aldlave exist at all? Academic Dr Judith A. Frost of the University of York, who has carried out extensive research into the story of the foundation of the order at Nostell, has been unable to find any contemporary record of a royal chaplain or a confessor called Ralph during the reign of Henry I.

As to the identity of the priory's founder, Dr Frost, writing in a Borthwick Paper entitled *The Foundation of Nostell Priory, 1109–1153*, discusses a number of candidates. These include, among others, Robert de Lacy, whose gift around 1106 of the woods in which the religious community made their home was referenced in the confirmation charter of Henry I, and Hugh de Laval, both of whom held the honour of Pontefract in the early twelfth century.

Dr Frost also refers to a record found in the medieval *Cartulary of Nostell Priory*, held by the British Library, which, she wrote, documents an agreement to provide 'the clerics of St Oswald' with a 'church and a cemetery for their use and the use of their servants at the place where they lived called Nostlet'. Interestingly, she also identified a clerk by the name of Ralph who was 'present with Robert I de Lacy at the dedication of the church of St Oswald by Archbishop Thomas II'. Thomas II was archbishop from 1109 to 1114. Was this church the 'old place' mentioned in *Gesta*? Was the clerk Aldlave? It is worth noting that at this time the community were regarded as clerics, rather than the Augustinian canons they would become. University of Oxford professors David Carpenter and Richard Sharpe, authors of the *Charters of William II and Henry I* project, wrote a 2013 paper dealing with Nostell's foundation. In this they declared that Ralph, 'did exist, and that he was leader of the clerks who served a chapel dedicated to St Oswald before the priory was established.' The same authorities also favour Thomas II, Robert de Lacy and cleric Ralph as the founders of Nostell, dating the foundation from 1108 to 1114. They suggest that the priory grew into a house of canons out of the chapel dedicated to St Oswald, which they tell us was 'dependent on Featherstone' (a nearby parish). They presume this chapel once stood where Wragby parish church is now situated. In other words, 'the old place'.

Other historians favour Thurstan, Archbishop of York, as the true founder of the Augustinian community at Nostell, or at least its 'major patron', offering 1114 (the year Thurstan became archbishop) to 1119 as the likely foundation period. This looks pretty sound, for in 1120 Thurstan was responsible for acquiring papal confirmation of the priory's foundation along with further endowments.

Whatever the 'true' story of the foundation, which seems to depend on exactly how 'day one' is defined, the canons remained at their priory in Nostell, thriving during the twelfth century, and the Act Book described how the site boasted '26 canons and 77 servants in the house' at this time. There were also servants to be found in the bakery, malthouse, brewhouse, smithy, and carpenter's shop, as well as employment for ploughmen and carriers.

In his South Yorkshire history, Hunter gave accounts of the successive Nostell priors, and of life at the priory during their reigns, including talk of the canons' rowdy annual feast, originally granted by Henry I, which was later suppressed because it had become an excuse for a yearly punch-up. He also described times of plenty, leaner pickings, contested elections of priors, and even the occasioning of grievous bodily harm!

'The Seal of Nostell Priory'.   The St Oswald coat of arms.

Dissolution

The bustling site remained a centre of monastic life until its dissolution in 1539, when it was conveyed to Thomas Legh.

Dr Legh played a major part in the legal process known as the Dissolution of the Monasteries, which took place from 1536 to 1540. This saw the suppression, asset-stripping and dismantling of English, Welsh and Irish religious houses, following the passing of the Act of Supremacy in 1534 and the Suppression of Religious Houses Act passed in February 1535/6. The earlier Act made Henry VIII supreme head of the Church of England following his break with Rome, whilst the later Act applied only to 'lesser houses' whose income was lower than £200 a year. The wording of the preamble of the Act of suppression suggested that 'Manifest sin, vicious, carnal and abominable living is daily used and committed amongst the little and small abbeys,' conveniently providing just cause for the closures that were carried out relatively smoothly, with little opposition.

This meant that proceeds from the closures, which saw monastic endowments and possessions transferred to the Crown, could swell the king's dwindling coffers without too many raised eyebrows. That said, risings and rebellions did take place, notably the Pilgrimage of Grace in 1536 in Yorkshire. But this was put down and the leaders were severely punished, Robert Aske, the rebellion's instigator, being executed for treason a year later.

Acting as an agent for the king, but reporting to the monarch's chief minister, Thomas Cromwell, Legh (often joined by the equally notorious Dr Richard Layton) was busy conducting visitations at monasteries, friaries, convents and priories, assessing their worth, reporting on the conduct of their officers and then dissolving them and pensioning off the heads of the houses.

When the end came for St Oswald's, the prior was a man named Robert Ferrar, whose name appears on the deed of surrender of St Oswald's, dated 20 November 1539. Hunter asserted that Ferrar 'must have been put in for the purpose of obtaining an easy surrender; for he was one of the most zealous of the reformers.' (Indeed, he would be burned at the stake in 1555 during the reign of Queen Mary.) Hunter assumed that the previous prior, a local man named Alvered Comyn, 'must have either died or resigned before the house was dissolved.' So what did happen to Prior Comyn?

Doctors Legh and Layton had made their visitation to Nostell during January 1535/6 and they sent a scandalous report concerning what they claimed to have found there. Hunter described their allegations as 'very gross crimes ... against several members ... by name' and he felt unable to 'give credit to the disgusting report of these visitors'.

This report, of which Hunter said no more, included claims that some of the canons had performed sodomy with young boys and that others had conducted affairs with local women. The charge against Prior Comyn was that he had been sharing his bed with two married women. Of course, it was Legh and Layton's task to find good reasons to close the priory. It couldn't be dissolved under the suppression of the lesser monasteries Act because it was reasonably wealthy, possessing a clear profit of £492 18s 1d in 1535. And so in these cases the 'discovery' of outrageous behaviour was not uncommon. Allegations were often extracted following intense, individual interviews with all the members of each house visited, including servants. Some of those grilled were keen to supply the visitors with what they wanted to hear, enjoying the opportunity to spread gossip about their colleagues and masters, and these testimonies, obviously exaggerated in many instances, helped to destroy the reputations of the houses. Legh was particularly noted for his heavy-handed approach to the task, often bullying and threatening the leaders of the monasteries he visited. In 1537, Thomas Howard, 3rd Duke of Norfolk (who was an uncle of Anne Boleyn), wrote a letter to Thomas Cromwell describing Legh as a 'vicious man'.

This ramping-up tactic exerted such pressure on the heads of the monasteries that it led to voluntary surrenders, many being afraid of what action might be brought against them if they resisted for too long.

In Nostell's case it would take Comyn's death in June 1538 before the priory could be 'voluntarily' ceded to the Crown a year later, with Robert Ferrar by then installed in the hot seat. A letter written in June 1538 from Sir John Nevyell to Dr Lee (presumably Dr Legh) stated: 'The prior of St Oswald's is dead and they are determined to keep it secret for three or four days, for what intent God knows, as I have certified my lord's Grace.'

Comyn had died shortly after Legh alone had made a second visit to Nostell in March 1538, when he found the old prior confined to his bed, extremely sick and 'powerless to stir hand or foot'. Legh, writing to Thomas Cromwell, revealed that he had urged Comyn to resign his office, 'as not able for the charge', but he refused to do so, talked out of it by 'a woman that kept him, and other kinsfolk living by him'.

Dead within weeks, no doubt brought to his end burdened with the knowledge of the inevitable loss of his priory, this was a sorry conclusion to Comyn's fourteen-year reign.

To speed matters along, a second Act of suppression, known as the Act for the Dissolution of the Greater Monasteries, was passed in 1539 and attention then turned to dissolving the remaining, wealthier institutions. Nostell's time was almost up; by November it was all over.

As for Prior Comyn, he is remembered today within Wragby parish church in the form of a great Latin inscription on the wall plate of the chancel, which instructs the onlooker to pray for the prior's soul, as it was he who built the choir 'in the ninth year of his priory, in the year of our Lord 1533', the original inscription reading:

Orate pro anima Alvredi Prioris, qui hunc chorum fieri fecit, anno sui prioratus nono, anno domini millesimo quingentesimo tricesimo tertio.

A collage showing the entire wall plate inscription that winds around the tops of the chancel walls.

The chancel wall bearing the inscription. This is a nineteenth-century copy of the original sixteenth-century wall plate.

Prior Comyn, in the middle panel in the window in Wragby parish church.

A stunning stained-glass window, originally installed in the east window of the church, depicting Prior Comyn, along with others who included Christ, the Virgin Mary and St Oswald, was observed by visiting antiquarian Roger

Dodsworth in September 1620 who poetically described Comyn's image as 'A man in a white gowne with a shaven crowne'. In around 1880, following restoration work carried out during the late eighteenth century and the 1820s, the surviving panels, including the middle panel of the lower tier that bore Comyn's image, were moved and placed in the church's 'golden window' above the vestry door. Today, Comyn can still be seen in his Augustine robes, looking over the congregation as he recites a Latin prayer.

Wolsey pays a visit

An interesting event in Nostell's history occurred during Comyn's time. As he had taken office in May 1524, he was prior when the famous Cardinal Wolsey visited Nostell in 1530. Wolsey was on his way to York, via Cawood, to be enthroned archbishop of the province, a fateful journey that he would never complete: he was arrested at Cawood and subsequently died at Leicester.

Before reaching Cawood, Wolsey spent a couple of days at St Oswald's, where he was kept busy confirming over 100 local children at the priory church. This notable occasion was described by Wolsey's usher, George Cavendish, who wrote an enlightening and lively biography of his master's life, which later inspired *Wolf Hall* author Hilary Mantel. In 1825, Samuel Weller Singer produced a complete edition of Cavendish's work in which he modernized the archaic mode of spelling, and within this version the account of the Cardinal's visit to Nostell is documented.

> Then about the feast of St Michael next ensuing my lord took his journey towards Cawood Castle, the which is within seven miles of York; and passing thither he lay two nights and a day at St Oswald's Abbey, where he himself confirmed children in the church, from eight of the clock in the morning until twelve of the clock at noon. And making a short dinner, resorted again to the church at one of the clock, and there began again to confirm more children until four of the clock, where he was at the last constrained for weariness to sit down in a chair, the number of the children was such. That done, he said his even song, and then went to supper, and rested him there all night. And the next morning he applied himself to depart towards Cawood; and or ever he departed, he confirmed almost a hundred children more; and then rode on his journey.

Font of the Priory of St Oswald at Nostel

The font from the
priory church.

Legh purchases the priory

On 22 March 1540, barely five months after its dissolution, the lease of the
priory was granted, by letters patent, to Dr Legh in return for the sum
of £1,126 13s 4d (1,690 marks). Hunter described the composition of the
'magnificent estate' that had been conveyed to Legh, as follows:

> The site of the priory, the whole church, bell-tower, and cemetery, with
> all messuages, granges, mills, houses, edifices, barns, dove-coats, gardens,
> orchards, &c. and sundry demesne lands … all mills in Wragby and
> Crofton; the grange of Huntwick, in the parish of Wragby, with the lands
> belonging to it; the capital messuage called Holewell, or Hovel-ball, in the
> parish of Thurnscoe, with a wood of 160 acres; the cell of Scokirk, with
> the church, bell-tower, cemetery &c.; and the manor of Bramham, called
> Bramham-Bigging, pasture for 360 sheep on the moors adjacent, rabbit-
> warren, wood, &c.; all late belonging to the priory.

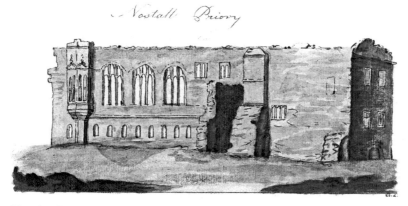

Sketch of part of the ruin of the Priory of St Oswald at Nostell.

Monks' Refectory, the only significant visible remains of the priory.

Following's Legh's death on 24 November 1545, his estate at Nostell, with other properties (Legh having divided his real estate into three parts in his will), passed to his 'loving wife', Joan, to 'fully and hooly remayne' to her for the 'terme of her lyfe to hir propre use and comoditie'.

Making provisions in his will for what should happen to his lands in the event of his wife's death, Legh added that 'if it chance me to dye w'out issue male of my body lawfully begotten' he wished to bequeath 'the two partes of all and singular my landes' (that he had bequeathed to his wife) to his nephew, also called Thomas Legh, and then to his nephew's heirs. Dr Legh's bequest was to include 'my mannor and howse of Sainte Oswaldes in Yorkshire with all the utensiles, necessaries, beddings, and all other implements of householde stuffe as it standith and is furnished at this present tyme'.

However, in the event that Joan gave birth to a son, Dr Legh stated that during the child's 'nonage' (childhood), the custody of these lands was to be shared between the following three men: Thomas Legh (the abovenamed nephew), Sir Edward North, and Thomas Gargrave. The last named gentleman was Legh's brother-in-law, who was married to Joan's sister, Anne Cotton, and would go on to play a major part in Nostell's story.

In the end, no son was born to this marriage, but Legh and his wife did already have a daughter, Catherine, who was five years old when the will was written. Her father left her 'a thousande markes toward hir mariage', which was equal to £666 13s 4d in old money.

Legh's widow Joan went on to marry statesman Sir Thomas Chaloner. In April 1554, Joan's nephew, Thomas Legh, conveyed his right to St Oswald's back to her. Joan died on 5 January 1557, and an inquest held at Pontefract determined that she was the rightful holder of St Oswald's (along with all the land described in the grant of 1540). At the same time, Joan's daughter Catherine was confirmed as her heiress and she duly inherited the estate.

Catherine Legh was quickly married off by her stepfather to James Blount, 6th Lord Mountjoy, a spendthrift who used much of his fortune to pursue an obsession with alchemy. This perhaps explains why, in 1568, the couple mortgaged and then sold Catherine's inheritance of the Nostell estate for £3,560. The purchasers were her uncle, the now knighted Sir Thomas Gargrave, who had recently been the speaker in the House of Commons, and his son, Sir Cotton Gargrave.

Here come the Winns

Nostell would subsequently pass through several hands. Its owners included Sirs John Wolstenholme senior and junior, both customs farmers, during whose tenure royalist statesman Edward Hyde, Earl of Clarendon, stayed 'concealed' at the house in 1642. Sir John Wolstenholme the younger also sympathized with the royalist cause during the Civil War years, and these sympathies were to lead to his financial ruin, to the extent that in 1654, Nostell was purchased by Rowland Winn, who quickly sold it to his brother, George. The Winns were successful London textile merchants, whose ancestral origins were rooted in Wales.

In 1660, as thanks for the support the Winns had shown to Charles II, the newly restored monarch, George Winn was made 1st Baronet of Nostel (as the title was spelled). During this period, the post-Dissolution house was known as Nostall Hall, and would remain standing until the late eighteenth century.

A seventeenth-century ground plan of 'Nostall Hall' shows that the surviving building incorporated three ranges from the main cloister of the original monastic house. Visiting a century earlier, Leland had described the house as 'exceding great and fair; and hath the goodlyest fontein of conduct water that is in that quarter of England.' It was established in an archaeological report in 2001 that Nostall Hall and St Oswald's Priory stood on land south-west of the present house. The Ordnance Survey map of 1892 correctly placed the priory here, showing the original priory, i.e. 'the old place', on the site of the present church, though the 2001 report suggested that there was no archaeological evidence for this particular designation.

In about 1736, the 1st Baronet's heir, Sir Rowland Winn, the 4th Baronet, would begin work on a magnificent new house in the Palladian style, which became the house known as Nostell Priory. Today it attracts thousands of visitors a year who come to see its impressive collection of paintings, Chippendale furniture and expansive parkland. Originally designed by Colonel James Moyser, the work was overseen, and in some parts redesigned, by the then teenage architect James Paine, who would go on to design the grand stables at Chatsworth House in Derbyshire.

But it is with the Gargrave family with whom the following tales begin, and in particular with Sir Thomas's wayward grandson and namesake, whose own father, Sir Cotton Gargrave, accused him of leading a 'a most loose, licentious, blasphemous, prowde, wastfull and contentious lief'.

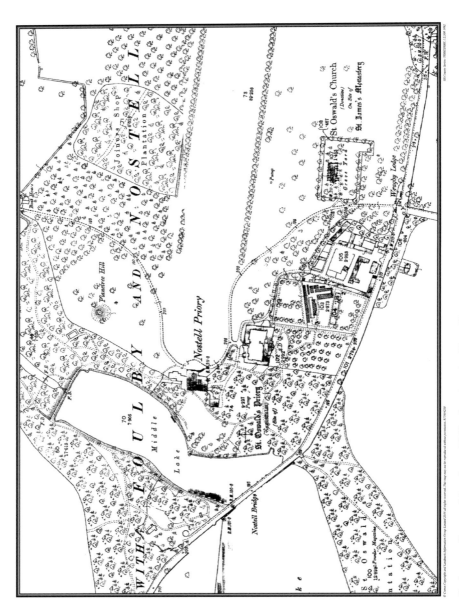

Ordnance Survey Map from 1892, showing the Nostell estate.

Chapter 1

The Gargraves

He is drowned into the forgetfulness of his duty to Almighty God and is fallen to a most loose, licentious, blasphemous, proud, wasteful and contentious life.

Sir Thomas

These were words from the will of Sir Cotton Gargrave of Nostell (c.1540–1588), two-time Member of Parliament for Boroughbridge during the 1570s, and in 1585 High Sheriff of Yorkshire. His father, Sir Thomas Gargrave (c.1495–1579), had purchased the Nostell estate in 1568 from his wife's niece, Lady Mountjoy, otherwise Catherine Blount, and had sat in Parliament several times since his first election in 1547 as the Member for York. In the first parliament of Queen Elizabeth in 1559, he held the office of Speaker of the House of Commons and is noted that year for suggesting to the queen that she marry, or as James J. Cartwright put it in *Chapters in the History of Yorkshire*, 'to request her, in the name of the nation, to be pleased to take a husband.'

A Wakefield family, who presumably originated from the village of Gargrave, near Skipton, where a John de Gayrgrave paid poll tax in 1379, the Wakefield Gargraves boasted among their ancestral ranks Sir John Gargrave. He was a tutor to the unfortunate Richard Plantagenet, the future Duke of York, who would meet a sticky end in December 1460 when he was relieved of his head at the Battle of Wakefield. Shakespeare's version of this event appears in *Henry VI, Part 3*, but it is in the first episode of the Bard's *Henry VI* trilogy that Sir John's own son, Sir Thomas Gargrave, appeared as a character, albeit a minor one. This Sir Thomas died childless during the Siege of Orléans of 1428–1429, and it was down to his brother, William, to continue the Gargrave line. Joseph Hunter, in his history of South Yorkshire, asserted that William was the great-great-grandfather of Sir Cotton himself, whose harsh words appeared in his will of 1585, words that referred to his own son, another Thomas Gargrave (c.1560–1595). We will discover later what had caused such interfamilial discord.

Sir Cotton's father, Sir Thomas, died on 28 March 1579 after a long life that began in about 1495 when he was born at Pear Tree Acres, located in the Old Park at Eastmoor, Wakefield. His year of birth is calculated from detail shown on a portrait in the National Portrait Gallery, which is dated 1570 and records that the sitter was seventy-five years of age at this time. He was twice married, firstly to Anne Cotton, whose sister was the wife of Dr Thomas Legh, the one-time possessor of the dissolved priory of St Oswald at Nostell, and then to Jane Appleton, the widow of John Wentworth of North Elmsall.

Sir Thomas was High Sheriff of Yorkshire twice in the 1560s, and vice president of the Council of the North at York before this. And in January 1569, he was involved in arranging the conveyance of the imprisoned Mary, Queen of Scots from Bolton Castle in Wensleydale, Yorkshire to Tutbury in Staffordshire. That same year, Sir Thomas also played a key role in the defeat of the Catholic earls of Northumberland (Thomas Percy) and Westmorland (Charles Neville) who had begun a rebellion with the objective of dethroning the protestant Queen Elizabeth to replace her with her cousin Mary, a devout Catholic. These events became known as the Rising of the North. During the campaign, Sir Thomas was tasked with defending the strategically important Pontefract Castle and the road running through nearby Ferrybridge in order to prevent the rebels reaching the city of York. He was mentioned in a letter sent to Queen Elizabeth at this time. It was written on 24 November 1569 by the Earl of Sussex, who assured the queen that 'Sir Thomas Gargrave is at Pomfret, and hath fortified the passage at Feribridg [Ferrybridge].'

Thomas wrote a series of letters of his own during the rising. One was addressed to George Talbot, 6th Earl of Shrewsbury, the powerful lord into whose custody the imprisoned Mary had been placed. It was written at Pontefract Castle on 25 November 1569, its contents revealing the outbreak of the rising and the knife-edge upon which the outcome was balanced, with a plea for the provision of men, money and lots of gunpowder.

My duty humbly remembered to your Lordship. Yester night the two Earls returned to Boroughbridge & called back all their companies & required them to repair from thence onwards towards the Forest of Galtres, as though they would go to York on the far side of [the] Ouse. They persuaded their soldiers to adventure to win York, where they may have gain & lay [during] the winter. And say, if they attain York all is theirs. And if they miss it, it were better for them to die like men than to be hanged. I fear not [for] York; it is strong enough to repulse them.

They were minded to have seized this house & to have wintered here & at Wakefield & at Doncaster, if they could have gotten them all. The only lack I fear here is money and gunpowder, whereof I would gladly have help for I cannot get any from York.

There cometh to serve the Queen a thousand light horsemen from the frontiers towards Scotland, and four hundred harquebuses [portable matchlock guns]. There cometh also from the south five hundred harquebuses & other munitions, which I look for to be here & to be conveyed to York within four or five days. And when the provision cometh I trust there will be a short end of the rebellion.

Pomfrett Castell [Pontefract Castle] the 25th of November 1569

In the end the rebels never reached York and their plans fell apart, the earls retreating towards Scotland. Northumberland was captured in 1572 and later beheaded, whilst Westmorland died in poverty in Flanders nearly thirty years later.

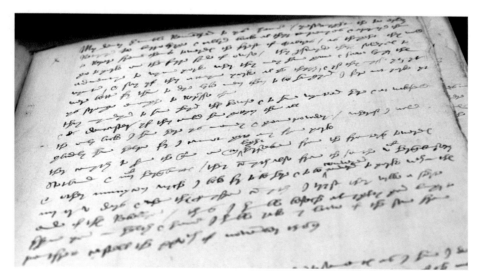

Thomas Gargrave's letter to George Talbot, 6th Earl of Shrewsbury.

PONTEFRACT CASTLE in the West Riding of YORKSHIRE.
Granted by WILLIAM the Conquerer to HILDEBERT de LASCY. Repaired by QUEEN ELIZABETH. but totally demolished in 1648. is thus transmitted to Posterity by the Society of Antiquaries, London. 1734.

Pontefract Castle.

As for Sir Thomas Gargrave, he survived the rising and lived for almost a decade more having acquired the several manors of Hemsworth, Wrenthorpe, Darton, Upton, Havercroft, Askern and, of course, Nostell. He prepared his last will on 27 March 1579, the day before he died. In it he recorded his desire to be buried within Wragby parish church, wishing for several sermons be read in his memory, stating:

If I make not a tomb before my death, then I will that my heirs or executors shall make one within six years next after my death, and I will that mention be thereon made of me and both my wives and of my children, and I will that [on] the day of my funerals there shall be a Sermon made by some learned man, and twelve more sermons to be made at Wragby Church on twelve of the next Sundays after my said funerals, and I will that other twelve sermons shall be made at Hemsworth Church on twelve Sundays next after the said twelve Sundays, that is to wit upon every of the twenty-four Sundays one sermon, in all which sermons I would have the people taught their duties in prayer, and in the commandments of God, and in charity towards their neighbours, and their justification by faith in Jesus Christ.

Whether or not these two-dozen sermons were read to the (hopefully) patient parishioners is not known, but Sir Thomas was indeed buried as he wished, his remains lying in the south choir of the church at Wragby. A tomb was duly erected and the inscription read:

Here lyeth Sir Thomas Gargrave, knight, who dyed the 28 of March, 1579, who served sundry times in the wars and as counsellor at Yorke xxxv yeare. He maryed Anne Cotton of Kent and Jane Appleton widow of Sir John Wenworth of Elmesall. He had issue only by Anne Cotton, two sonnes, Cotton and John, which John dyed att his byrth.

The reference to Hemsworth church appeared in the will because Sir Thomas possessed Kinsley Hall, which was situated within the parish of Hemsworth. To the 'inhabitants of everie cottaige' in the two parishes of Wragby and Hemsworth, he left twelve pence. He also bequeathed a quarter of wheat and another of rye to the 'poore of Wragbie', and this was to be

Sir Thomas Gargrave, by unknown artist, oil on panel, 1570.

delivered to their houses on the day of the funeral. After detailing further acts of charity, Sir Thomas declared his wish for his wife Jane to remain at the family seat at Nostell, stating:

> considering my wife's age and impotency, and by reason of her age, the decay of sight and hearing, I do will and desire her my said wife to remain in house with my son or other my heir during her life, and that she shall have convenient chambers and lodgings with beds, fires and other necessaries, for herself, her two maids, and one man. And for her chamber, if she like, the chamber wherein she now lies, that then she shall have and keep the same with the two chambers next within the same with the bed clothes and therein and convenient meat and drink for her, and her said servants; and I will that my heirs shall pay her fifty pounds rents yearly at Pentecost and Martinmas

Sir Thomas's concern for the fate of his wife was illustrated in a further passage in his will addressed directly to his son Cotton, entreating him to look after his stepmother:

I charge my son even as the father may charge the son before God, that he be gentle and good unto her as unto his father's good wife as he hath good cause, if he call to remember her rare diligence and goodness towards him in his youth, and her kindness now to his children.

The testator's grandson, Thomas Gargrave, though not specifically mentioned in the will, was about eighteen or nineteen years of age at this time. And a year after his grandfather's death, the majority of his father Cotton's newly inherited estates, including Nostell, Kinsley and Upton, were entailed in his favour. This meant that when Sir Cotton came to rewrite his own will in 1585, disinheriting Thomas was not option.

Like his own father, Sir Cotton had been married twice, firstly to Bridget Fairfax, with whom he had Thomas and two other sons – Robert, who died aged seventeen, and John, who died in infancy – and secondly to Agnes Waterton, of Walton Hall, who bore Sir Cotton several children including their son Richard Gargrave, and five daughters.

Sir Cotton's eldest son, Thomas, had entered St John's College at the University of Cambridge as a fellow-commoner in 1573, apparently at the age of twelve or thirteen, his fellow-commoner status meaning he was entitled to dine with the other fellows of the same college. There is no record of his graduation, which perhaps isn't surprising for Thomas was somewhat of a loose cannon.

Not long after this, and certainly before January 1575/6, Sir Cotton, his father Sir Thomas, and James Pilkington, Bishop of Durham, had agreed that the bishop's daughter Deborah would marry Sir Cotton's son Thomas, who was presumably still enrolled at Cambridge. Writing in his will, dated 21 January 1575/6, the bishop referred to the impending betrothal and in particular to a penalty that Sir Cotton and his father would have to forfeit should the intended groom 'refuse to taike my sayde doughter Debora to his wyfe'. The sum in question was a huge £700 that had been settled on the Gargraves by the bishop to secure the marriage, plus a further £100 out of their own pockets 'to the preferment of the marriage of the sayd Debora'. In the end the marriage never took place, and young Deborah stood to receive the entire sum 'payde to her owne use'. The story of what happened next will show that the bishop's daughter got off very lightly indeed!

Thomas the terrible

To suggest that Sir Cotton Gargrave was in an ill mood when he sat down on 31 January 1585/6 to draft a new version of his last will and testament would be quite the understatement. The words that poured out onto the pages before him illustrated his feelings towards his eldest son in no uncertain terms. The document, perhaps drawn up by Edward Beckwith, Sir Cotton's servant who is known to have drawn up at least one other document, begins with a reference to an earlier will made on 25 October 1582. Of this former will, Sir Cotton says he had made his son Thomas his executor for the 'good affection I did then bear unto him'; good affection that, by January 1585/6, had evidently turned sour.

Sir Cotton declared that his son was 'drowned into the forgetfulness of his duty to Almighty God', owing to 'his most intolerable and monstrous pride'. Such pride had caused Thomas to lead a 'most loose, licentious, blasphemous, proud, wasteful and contentious life', to the 'destruction of his own estate, body and soul'. Cotton further alleged that his son was 'suspected of unnatural attempts against father, mother, brethren and sisters, contrived in his most wicked and proud mind'. But what terrible acts of depravity had Thomas been attempting, exactly? The answer, it seems, was cold-blooded murder!

According to the will, Thomas Gargrave had purchased poison from an apothecary in London and together with a Frenchman had mixed the poison into a 'mease of pottage in his lodging' and fed it to a dog who subsequently died. William Carr defines the word mease in his 1828 publication *The Dialect of Craven: in the West-Riding of Yorkshire* as a measure of something, e.g. meat, and the phrase 'mease of pottage' appears in *Two Twinnes*, written in 1613 by Richard Bernard, a Puritan clergyman, as an analogy for something of no value, i.e. a low quality dish. Sir Cotton insisted that his son had not denied the charge when it was made 'in the presence of Mr Gervase Neville esquire, Mr Robert Bradford esquire [a local justice of the peace], Mr John West esquire, Edward Beckwith and Anthony Reynold'. Sir Cotton also alleged that his son 'rewarded my cook and butler at that time more than he did in all his life before and quarrelled with my trustiest friends and servants.' The offences that Sir Cotton levelled against his son and one-time heir dominated the will and he concluded by making it clear that he wanted nothing more to do with Thomas.

He hath behaved towards my wife most ungodly and undutifully I finding him given over unto all these devilish practices and never in my life finding him natural or loving towards me but trusting that riper years would have bred better friends in him, but now seeing his more monstrous activities growing from worse to worse … he [is] overawed with such pride that he forgets his duty to God and nature.

Therefore, I respecting the good gift of God bestowed upon me, and the dutiful and natural love that I bear towards my wife, Lady Anne Gargrave, and her children by me begotten, not minding to put any trust, or bestow any part of my goods or the execution thereof upon so lewd a person as Thomas Gargrave, to maintain his sin and wickedness, but do hereby renounce and make void my former will and leave it cancelled and defaced, the seals pulled off and my name subscribed erased. And that former will and every part thereof void whereof the said Thomas is appointed my executor, [I do] hereby debar him from the execution or intermeddling with any part of my goods. And do make this my last will and testament in manner and form following.

What did follow was Sir Cotton's wish to be buried at Wragby church and for his name to be mentioned on the brass that appeared on the tomb he had built for his father. He referred to the will made by his late father and hoped that it would be performed. And after payment of his debts had been made, Sir Cotton left 1,000 marks each to his daughters, Anne, Mary, Elizabeth and Priscilla, upon their eighteenth birthdays, or on their wedding days if they came sooner, 'and the like to the child my wife is [pregnant] with, if a daughter'. The child in question was indeed a daughter, whom Sir Cotton and Lady Anne named Frances. Lady Anne replaced Thomas as the executor of the will but before he signed and sealed the document, the testator had one last complaint to lay at his son's door. It concerned Thomas's time at Cambridge in the 1570s. Sir Cotton cautioned his wife not to give any trust to her stepson, who had 'forgotten his duty towards me … [and] the great care I had of his bringing up in learning the space of eight years to my extreme charges.' Crying poverty during the early days of his second marriage, Sir Cotton claimed that all he'd had to live on when he sent his son to university was 'but four score pounds yearly from my father for me and my whole family'. Yet despite this, Sir Cotton pointed out that he had bestowed upon Thomas 'yearly, forty, fifty, and threescore pound at Cambridge'. Presumably, he felt this had been an utter waste of money.

Finally, ending his will, Sir Cotton doubted that any son had treated a father in a worse manner, but hoped that God would grant his son grace so that he might mend his sinful ways.

Sir Cotton lived until 16 June 1588, long enough to see his wayward son married to Catherine Wentworth, daughter of Thomas Wentworth of Wentworth Woodhouse. Their marriage took place shortly after 26 January 1587, on which date Thomas Gargrave and Miss Catherine Wentworth were named in a lease whereby they conveyed 'certain messuages, lands, coal mines and rents' to Sir Cotton, by way of a marriage settlement.

Contrary to almost all other accounts, the couple went on to have not one, but three daughters, whom they called Margaret, Anne and Prudence. The youngest, Prudence, was baptized at Wragby on 5 November 1592, but not before a series of legal proceedings had taken place between Thomas and his stepmother, Lady Gargrave, concerning arguments over ownership of family land.

Letters survive that describe these feuds. On 27 July 1589, George Talbot, 6th Earl of Shrewsbury, wrote from Sheffield to William Cecil, Lord Burghley, who was Lord High Treasurer at the time, asking for help on Lady Gargrave's behalf. Shrewsbury wrote that he was 'being moved with compassion towards the poor Lady Gargrave and her great charge of younger children whose estate is like to become much lessened through those suits wherewith her son-in-law [i.e. Thomas Gargrave, this being an alternative term for stepson] doth daily molest her.' Early the following year, Roger Manners, a personal attendant to Queen Elizabeth, wrote to Shrewsbury enclosing a letter by Sir Francis Walsingham, spymaster and the Chancellor of the Duchy of Lancaster, in which he ordered the earl to settle the feud between the Gargraves.

If Shrewsbury managed to smooth relations then the peace did not last, for just a few years later, Thomas Gargrave found himself in serious trouble. He was arrested and charged with murder and later with escaping from custody, charges that would bring about an abrupt end to his life.

The exact events concerning the murder for which Thomas was indicted have long been shrouded in mystery, Reverend Hunter providing a vague account in his South Yorkshire opus. Hunter repeated a claim made by

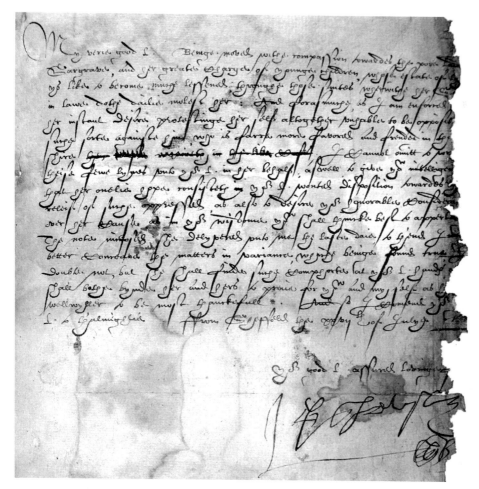

A letter from the Earl of Shrewsbury to Lord Burghley, Lord Treasurer, dated 27 July 1589, sent on behalf of Lady Gargrave, Sir Cotton's widow.

seventeenth-century antiquarian Roger Dodsworth, who, writing not more than forty years after the supposed murder had taken place, had suggested that Thomas Gargrave had been found guilty of poisoning a young servant boy whose dead body he'd then burned in an oven! This horrific tale is still told at Nostell Priory at Halloween to scare visitors, despite the fact that Dodsworth and Hunter specifically said that the murder had taken place not at Nostell but at Kinsley, where the Gargraves also held land. Evidence shows that they were (and still are) all mistaken.

On 15 July 1594, indictments brought against Thomas Gargrave were, as Hunter correctly stated, 'certified into the Court of King's Bench'. This court sat at Westminster Hall and the records of its proceedings are kept at The National Archives at Kew. Within these records, which in those days were written entirely in Latin, the very indictments Hunter referred to can be found, though he admitted he had not actually seen them. Hunter, and others after him, wrote of how Gargrave had poisoned his servant, 'a poor man' who went by the name 'Gardyner'. Citing Dodsworth, Hunter said that the 'charge was for *poisoning and burning a boy of his kitchen in the oven.*' What a brute! Brutish, and indeed callous, are words that might justifiably be levelled at Thomas Gargrave, but a burner of young boys' bodies? Well, following a quick look at the indictments, it would appear not.

The specifics of the two charges brought against Gargrave were that he had absconded while held in the prison at York Castle, where he'd been detained on suspicion of murdering one John Gardiner of Hemsworth. According to the indictment for murder, the charge was heard at York Sessions Justice of the Peace court, where the shocking circumstances of what actually happened were relayed.

Apparently, on 1 May 'in the thirty-third year of the reign of our lady Elizabeth, by the grace of God queen of England, France, and Ireland, defender of the faith &c.', or 1 May 1591, to be precise, Thomas Gargrave, 'seduced by devilish prompting, from his malice aforethought, slyly, warily, devilishly, and feloniously intending death' offered a 'certain beaker of wine' to a yeoman farmer named John Gardiner (otherwise Gardyner) of Hemsworth. The wine had been 'made up beforehand with a certain poison called *marcure sublimate*', in other words, sublimated mercury, that is to say, ground mercury rendered into powder. The cup had been proffered, and the indictment is very clear about this, while the pair were at York Castle. What they were doing there is unclear. Hustings that took place prior to elections were held at the castle but there was no election that year, so it's possible that both men were in prison at the time, though this seems unlikely, given the access to wine and poison. Gargrave 'prompted' Gardiner to take the wine, which he did, taking the cup 'into his hands then and there and accepted, drank, and drained the aforesaid wine, thus poisoned as above ... not knowing that the aforesaid wine had been mixed with poison.'

It wasn't long before the poison took effect, and Gardiner 'fell ill and languished, from the first day of May aforesaid ... until the twenty-fifth day of October in the abovesaid year.' In other words, the unfortunate John Gardiner made it back to Hemsworth and died there on 25 October 1591 'from the said draught and by reason of poisoning thereof in the manner and from aforesaid'. The indictment ends with little doubt as to the assembled jurors' verdict. They found Gargrave guilty.

and so the jurors aforesaid say that the aforesaid Thomas Gargrave feloniously, wilfully, and of his malice aforethought killed and murdered the aforementioned John Gardyner, wilfully and feloniously, with the poison aforesaid in the manner and form aforesaid, against the peace of the said lady, now queen, her crown and dignity, and against the form of statute issued and provided in a case of this sort

So Thomas Gargrave's victim, like the poor dog we learned about in his father's will, had met his death, not by being baked alive, but as a result of Gargrave's favoured modus operandi: poisoning. Unless, that is, the small matter of Gardiner having been bundled into an oven at Kinsley and then cremated, had been omitted from the indictment as not relevant to the case.

We know that Prudence, Thomas's daughter, was born and baptized at Wragby a year after Gardiner's demise, while, presumably, her father remained at liberty. His initial arrest, then, must have taken place after this.

The second indictment reveals that Gargrave was initially charged with the murder some two and half years after Gardiner's death, on 10 May 'in the thirty-sixth year ... of the said lady Elizabeth', that being 1594, when he was committed to prison back at York Castle. Despite the supposed safe custody in which he was kept, Gargrave made loose on 3 July that year, travelling '*ad loca incognita*', i.e. 'to places unknown', before being recaptured in London, from where he was returned to York for trial. Found guilty on both counts, there was only one sentence Gargrave could have expected, and it's the one he received: death.

He would have to wait until the following year to be put out of his misery, when on 16 June he was taken to the gallows on the Knavesmire, now part of York racecourse, and hanged from the neck until he was dead.

Thomas Gargrave's daughter would later protest her father's innocence, writing an account of these sorry events in a manuscript, which, according to Hunter, was titled *The case of Prudence Gargrave*. In this she claimed:

> Gardyner, who was supposed to be poisoned, was a poor man, Mr Gargrave's servant, and had all his means from him. He could gain nothing by his death. And it is to be proved by men yet living, that by reports of surgeons [*chirurgions* in the original text], who saw him and had him in care, that he died not of poisoning, but of a disease called a noli-me-tangere.

This seems like wishful thinking given the precise wording of the indictment for the murder, which had taken place before Prudence had been born. And, owing to the entail, Nostell passed not to her but to her father's male heir, his half-brother, Richard Gargrave, who was Prudence's uncle, so she was obviously a little miffed, to say the least. Furthermore, we may turn to another source in which the wily ways of wicked Thomas Gargrave are referred.

In 1604 at the age of forty-five, widower Sir William Wentworth, of Wentworth Woodhouse, began writing a handbook containing advice to his 22-year-old son and heir, Sir Thomas Wentworth. Sir William was Thomas Gargrave's brother-in-law (Gargrave's wife, Catherine, being Sir William's sister), and the older man was keen to use the pages of the handbook to tell his son all about his late relative, who in this document comes across as a paranoid, scheming psychopath.

> I trust he died in a better mind, being executed at York upon an indictment for poisoning one Gardiner, his man, and also for breach of prison, being committed for felony. At that time the Earl of Huntingdon [Henry Hastings, the 3rd Earl] was president of the Council at York [the Council of the North] and lieutenant of the shire, who hated Gargrave mortally. I have heard that at the gallows he protested himself clear for Gardiner's death, but his breach of prison, being committed for felony, was in extremity felony. True it is that I dare never keep him company, though he remained many days at my father's house, and he bearing no goodwill to me ... The causes why I might neither trust him, nor keep company with

him, were the experience I had of his most dangerous nature and subtlety in his imagined plots, though by protestations and letters he laboured exceedingly to insinuate himself into my good opinion and company.

Wentworth continued this appraisal of his less than affable brother-in-law by recalling the dramatic events described in Sir Cotton's will, while adding some spicy details of his own.

It was well known that once he bought poison and tried it upon a dog; again it is well known that he distilled poisons and kept them in glasses. His father, Sir Cotton Gargrave being a man very wise, believed even to his last gasp that he was by him most impiously empoisoned, as appears also in his last will of record at York. His two innocent daughters [Thomas Gargrave's daughters], being about three and four years old, died upon very few days' sickness and both on one day, or within twenty-four hours together, both having ulcers alike in their heads. Sir Cotton had a hole in the breast under the pap whereof he died. This man's most strange courses with his wife I omit, being weary to call to mind too many of these things, but that I may show good reason why I refused his company. For I like not to judge any man, neither to speak ill of the dead. But I pray God have mercy of his soul and ours too, amen.

Thomas Gargrave's elder daughters, Margaret and Anne, generally omitted from most histories of this family, were indeed buried at Wragby within a couple of days of one another, on 2 and 4 November 1591 respectively, just a month after Gardiner's demise. This proves Wentworth's testimony that the young girls had died within a short time of each other. It should be noted that Margaret had been baptized in 1590, so wasn't quite as old as Wentworth had thought, but he was writing several years after these events.

Perhaps by way of a cruel irony, Sir Thomas Wentworth, nephew of Thomas Gargrave, would also be executed by the state, his head removed by the blow of an axe on 12 May 1641. Sir Thomas, then 1st Earl of Strafford, had supported Charles I against Parliament, and paid the ultimate price for his loyalty, the king signing his death warrant in an act he would recall with great regret at the precise moment of his own execution in 1649. Among the

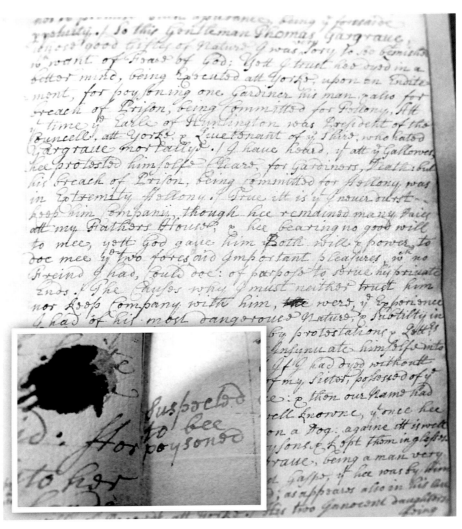

A page from Sir William Wentworth's 1604 book of advice to his son Thomas.

last words he uttered, the king declared that God was punishing him for 'an unjust sentence that I suffered to take effect'.

Catherine Gargrave, Thomas's wife, never remarried, remaining his widow for thirty-six years before her own death in 1631. Her only surviving daughter, Prudence Gargrave, who would become the wife of Oliver Cromwell's physician, Dr Richard Berry, placed a monument in Hemsworth parish church dedicated to the memory of her mother, which in part reads:

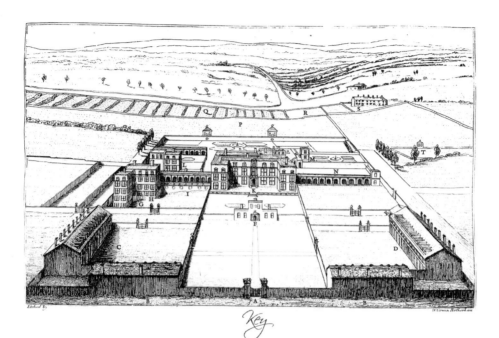

A - The Principal Entry
B - Two Stables
C - Brewhouse, Bakehouse, etc
D - A Stable
E - Coach-house and Stable
F - Porter's Lodge
G - A Tower
H - The Kitchen
I - Vaults, over which is the passage
    from the hall to the kitchen

K - The House
L - Another Tower, with lodgings
M - Banquetting House and lead walks
N - An Orangery
O - Two Summer Houses
P - A Grove
Q - The Orchard
R - The Kitchen Garden
S - The Gardener's House
T - The Bowling Green

Wentworth Woodhouse as it looked in William Wentworth's time, prior to the erection of the magnificent house that stands in its place today. From Hunter's *South Yorkshire*.

To the happie and perpetual memory of her dear and ever honored mother, Catharin, late wife to Thomas Gargrave sonn and heire to Sr Cotton Gargrave. of Nosthall, in the county of Yorke, knight: daughter to Thomas Wentworth, of Wentworth-Woodhouse, Esquire ... interred in the same grave with Briget, her mother-in-law, first wife of the said Sir Cotton ... She [Catherine] lived in wedlock eight years with her said husband; and remayned his mournfull widdow thirty and six yeares; spending her dayes religiously to God, hospitable towards her friends, and charitable towards all: and deceased the sixt day of October, 1631, leaveing issue to condole her want, her onely daughter and heyre Prudence Gargrave, by whom this monument was erected – Humble in prosperitie, Constant in adversitie, rarely exemplar in both fortunes.

One wonders if Prudence ever knew of the existence of her unlucky sisters. Her uncle and the heir to Nostell, Sir Richard Gargrave, through the failure of his brother's male line and state execution, inherited at least eleven manors, and later assumed the office of High Sheriff of Yorkshire. He was also Member of Parliament for Aldborough and then Yorkshire.

Richard Gargrave's fortune was valued at £3,500 a year, but he blew his riches through extravagance and fast living. Hunter wrote that he was 'fond of the midnight revel, and devoted to play', whilst a mini biography of Gargrave in the *History of Parliament* book series states that he was 'addicted to drinking, gambling and extravagance'. One particularly vivid image that appears in most accounts of Richard Gargrave's life suggests that even as his debts mounted up, he was prone to riding the streets of Wakefield throwing money at the hard-up natives. Ultimately so indebted, he was forced to break the Nostell entail, and on 23 June 1613 he sold the estate to one Francis Ireland, thus ending the Gargraves' possession of Nostell Priory.

As for Richard's fate after this, he is rumoured to have died penniless in London, 'found dead', according to Hunter, 'in an old hostelry, with his head upon a pack-saddle.' His burial, on 28 December 1638, appears in the parish registers of the Church of St Bartholomew the Great in London, the entry reading: 'Sir Richard Gargrave, knight was buried.'

The Gargrave monument in the north aisle of St Helen's church, Hemsworth.

From here the Gargraves slipped into obscurity, and Lord Byron is thought to have brought the family's fortunes to mind when he wrote the following lines, which appear in his poem *On Ancient Greece*.

Twere long to tell, and sad to trace,
Each step from splendour to disgrace

Sir Cotton's debt to the Crown

There is one final footnote to this family's story. When Sir Cotton Gargrave died in June 1588, he owed over £1,000 to the Crown ('one thousand one hundred fourscore and seventeen pounds, fourteen shillings, eight pence and half a penny-farthing' to be exact). This money had been collected while Sir Cotton was carrying out his duties as receiver of revenues for the Duchy of Lancaster in Pontefract, Knaresborough, Tickhill and Wakefield, and the sum also comprised revenues from the chantries in York – money he'd never handed over. In order to raise funds to recover the sum, the queen set up a commission to investigate the matter with powers to seize goods from the Gargrave estates amounting to the same value as the debt. Documents relating to the matter, held within the collections of The National Archives, record that the commissioners, Martyne Byrkette, Henry Slingsby and Stephen Harvey, 'repaired to Nostell in the county of York, the late house of Sir Cotton Gargrave, knight deceased,' and there 'examined' Edward Beckwith, Sir Cotton's servant, who had been responsible for physically collecting the revenues that should have been paid to the Crown. Sir Cotton's widow, Lady Gargrave, was also examined. The commissioners reported back to the queen, telling her that Beckwith and Lady Gargrave had claimed that some months before he'd died, Sir Cotton had instructed Beckwith to draw up a deed gifting all his goods and chattels to his five daughters. Clearly seeing this as an attempt to worm their way out of handing over the cash, the commissioners did not hold back when recording what they thought of the answers given to them by Lady Gargrave and Edward Beckwith (pretended in the sense used below meant ventured):

We have taken the examination of the Lady Agnes Gargrave widow and late wife of the said Sir Cotton and of the said Edward Beckwith for and concerning one deed of gift of all the goods and chattels of the said Sir Cotton pretended to be made unto his five daughters as by their several examinations herein enclosed

And we have also received from the said Lady Gargrave a copy of one inventory being delivered unto us by the said Lady as a note of her children's goods pretended to be given to them by the said Sir Cotton and praised by certain persons whose names are subscribed to the original remaining which the said Lady Gargrave and by us examined and cast down to the sum of £1,819 5s 8d.

Beckwith probably didn't help his cause when he admitted under oath that he couldn't remember on what day, in which month or even during what year he'd written up this mysterious deed, which he couldn't show to the commissioners because it had been sealed and delivered to a chap named Waterhouse for safekeeping in the presence of certain people 'whose names he doth not now well remember'. When it was her turn to be questioned, Lady Gargrave was able to furnish the commissioners with a little more detail concerning the deed of gift, recalling 'certain words' that appeared in it, which made her think, though she couldn't be sure, that it had been drawn up some time between Michaelmas 1587 (29 September) and Candlemas 1588 (2 February). She did recall that these gifts for her daughters were for 'their bringing up and education as [well as] for their advancement in marriage'. Lady Gargrave admitted that her husband sold 'threescore oxen' to a bloke named Marshall for just over £200 around the time of the deed being drawn up, but she couldn't remember whether or not this was before or after the deed was made.

When summing up their findings, the commissioners stated that Lady Gargrave had confessed to withholding certain 'other goods and sums of money ... [which] we have added unto the said inventory'. This inventory, detailing the goods, chattels and cattle supposedly given to the daughters of Sir Cotton and Lady Gargrave, is dated 8 July 1588 and forms part of the material gathered by the commissioners. It survives at The National Archives and its contents paint a fascinating picture of the household of Sir Cotton and his family. A copy of the inventory appears in the appendix of this book and it is well worth a look.

Chapter 2

The Coming of the Winns

The year of the Restoration of the English monarchy – 1660 – also saw the new owner of Nostell, George Winn, created 1st Baronet of Nostel by King Charles II. Winn's heirs would develop the estate by adding the present house in the eighteenth century, holding on to it until 1953, when the property was sold as a tourist attraction.

It was the 4th Baronet, Sir Rowland Winn, who built the new house, engaging Colonel James Moyser as principal architect, and teenager James Paine as interior designer and head of works.

In 1727, Sir Rowland had returned to England from a Grand Tour, his head brimming with ideas for a brand new, splendid residence to dwarf what remained of Nostall Hall, though the old building would be retained to house servants until it was demolished in the 1770s. During his travels Sir Rowland visited Italy, and it is therefore unsurprising that the house he envisaged, inspired by what he saw on his travels, was ultimately built in the style of Andrea Palladio, a sixteenth-century Italian architect. Writing in the scarce *Nostell Collection*, an early twentieth-century book prepared for the Winn family that catalogues the house's art collections, author and art historian Maurice Brockwell confirmed that the house was based on a design seen during Winn's 'travels on the Continent'.

A couple of years after his return, Sir Rowland married Susanna Henshaw at Lincoln's Inn Chapel in London. Susanna, a descendant of Sir Thomas More, was the daughter and co-heiress of Charles Henshaw, a London merchant. She would bear Rowland eight surviving children; the need for a new, larger house perhaps made ever more urgent by all these arrivals. It would be built, from about 1736, close to the old priory, Brockwell explaining that:

> It was erected near the site of the old Priory, its situation being rather elevated in the midst of a fertile and well cultivated tract of country. The Principal

Front is to the East, of great length, and extended by two wings of irregular form [one since demolished]. The centre is ornamented with a pediment, displaying the arms of the family finely sculpted and supported by a hexastyle of Ionic columns. The windows are regularly decorated. The basement is rustic [containing fragments of the monastic building], with an ascent of many steps on the exterior of the principal floor.

The West Front is composed of a pilastrade, also supported by a rustic basement. Each vestibule, the rooms appropriated to the servants' use, and the backstairs to the top of the house, are finished with ashlar stone regularly pointed. The same exactness is preserved in the upright joints of the ashlar in all the fronts, all the material being of the best kind.

Brockwell's book also contains interesting architectural plans, one of which was submitted by Paine showing his plan for the principal floor.

Several years later, in 1776, Robert Adam, the famous neoclassical British architect, erected the second of the irregular wings described above by Brockwell, and the image opposite illustrates how they appeared during the nineteenth century. Originally, Adam planned to erect four new wings, but ultimately only the one shown on the right of the image survives.

Adam had been hired by the 5th Baronet, also called Sir Rowland Winn, who had succeeded to the estate on the death of his father, the 4th Baronet, in 1765. Being a vain and extravagant man, the new owner wasn't happy with the house as it was left to him and so set about initiating bigger and bolder plans.

Nine years earlier, while living and studying in Vevey in Switzerland, the then 17-year-old Rowland had met and fallen in love with the married daughter of a rich Swiss banker, whom the young man had been introduced to. His subsequent relationship with Sabine Louise May, née d'Hervart, five years his senior, would prove highly controversial, but these events would set in motion a most colourful period in Nostell's history.

Rowland and Sabine's relationship had begun soon after the young man had arrived in Vevey with his tutor in August 1756. And though she was already married it was widely known that Sabine did not cohabit with her husband, Gabriel May. Even so, Sabine's and Rowland's romance was very much an on/off affair to begin with – one that Rowland's father, the 4th Baronet, had come to hear about. Attempting to calm matters, Rowland's tutor, Isaac Dulon, wrote to the 4th Baronet that October to

The present house shown in 1829, from J.P. Neale's *Views of the seats, Mansions, Castles etc. of Noblemen and Gentlemen in England, Wales, Scotland and Ireland*. The 4th Baronet, whose grand vision lay behind this stunning building, is also noted for the small role he played during the crushing of the Jacobite rebellion of the 1740s. It was he who suspected that Dr John Burton, the physician and antiquarian writer whose work we touched upon earlier, was sympathetic to the Jacobite cause. In the end no conviction was secured against Burton, who had left the city of York (where he practised) in November 1745, heading towards Lancashire, where he was later arrested, having been seen in the company of the rebels.

assure him that the affair had petered out and come to an end. But that was simply not true.

The academic, Christopher Todd, wrote a paper about Sabine Winn in 2005 for the *Yorkshire Archaeological and Historical Society*. He explained that Rowland and Dulon had moved on to Lausanne by November 1756, from where Dulon sent accounts back to the 4th Baronet at Nostell that revealed Rowland's lavish spending habits on items such as 'clothes, jewellery, furniture and paintings'. Todd continued:

he always liked to have fresh flowers in his rooms, and paid for musicians to come and play for him. Apparently dressing like a jockey while in Lausanne, through his landlord he also developed his lifelong passion for trading in horses.

In a letter to his father dated 15 October 1756, Rowland acknowledged that his accounts might contain 'expenses which you may not approve of', and was sorry Dulon hadn't written about these sooner but the tutor had 'got a swelling in his hand and it is impossible for him write.' Rather nonchalantly, Rowland hoped his father would not mind that he had 'bought some horses'.

Things changed dramatically for Rowland when, following a year's illness, Sabine's husband died of cancer in March 1759. And a month later, Rowland instructed Dulon to inform his father of his wish to marry the widow, with whom he was now besotted. The 4th Baronet responded with his own letter telling Rowland, in no uncertain terms, to reconsider, including a list of exactly why his son must not take this foreigner to be his wife.

His first reason referred to the fact that Sabine was 'several years older' than Rowland, and he was quick to the point out that this disparity seldom rendered a happy marriage, especially when the 'young man' was, in Rowland's case, in his twenties. Secondly, he advised against marrying 'an alien unacquainted with the language, customs and manners of the English nation which you must have observed to be very different from those of other countries.' He pursued this line of thinking with his next objection, insisting that because Sabine had no connection with a family in England with whom she could make a friend, the couple would instead make 'many enemies'. Presumably, Rowland's father imagined the pair's peers directing racism and discrimination at them.

No, Rowland's choice of bride just wouldn't do, and his father told him to choose 'a proper wife in your own country' so that he would always have connections with persons 'that may often be of service'. The baronet then questioned how genuine his son's feelings actually were, calling their relationship a 'pretended attachment' that could be 'nothing more than that of indulging a silly idle passion without thought or reflection'. He pointed out that Sabine's first husband was barely cold and yet all of a sudden, 'thoughts of marrying his widow come into your head.' If he'd only take a moment to think about it, then Sir Rowland was convinced his son would 'be of the same opinion as myself that she will be a very improper person for a wife for my son.' And if Sabine was 'a woman of sense', she too would come to the same conclusion. The 4th Baronet urged young Rowland to try to picture his foreign bride at the head of the table in refined English company. Conjure that image and he'd soon realize she'd be the subject of utter ridicule.

'How often have I heard and seen you laughing [at] or mimicking a Frenchman ... speaking English?' asked the 4th Baronet. 'Will you like to hear and see any person laughing [at] or mimicking your wife?' he continued. 'And if they do it before your face you must expect they will do it behind your back.'

These words had their desired effect, for a while at least, for Rowland took a step back from the relationship. But not for long; his aching heart strings soon pulled him back to Sabine.

Plans of marriage quickly returned to the forefront of his mind and in April 1761 he wrote to his father from Vevey, pouring his heart out, desperate to close the deal and become a married man. He told his father that 'it is impossible for me to express to you the great acknowledgement I have for all which you are so good as to do for me.' Rowland was referring to the fact that his father had reluctantly accepted that the argument was lost and was now working hard to secure a beneficial marriage settlement from Sabine's parents, the d'Hervart family. This was despite their reluctance to send part of their fortune to England. Clearly the 4th Baronet had softened in his stance for his son also wrote that 'it is certain that you have done for me what a most tender and perfect father could ever do for his son,' and the younger man was desperate to convince his father that nothing could equal the contentment and happiness he felt at that moment.

'Madame May,' the younger man wrote, 'is very sensible of the letter you have been so good as to write to her, and endeavours to assure you of it in a second letter which she writes today without communicating it to anybody but myself.' He continued:

I hope [Sabine's letter] will convince you of her perfect acknowledgment for so great a favour, and am thoroughly persuaded that when she will have the advantage of being known to you, you will grant the same esteem and attachment as for your own daughter. I will beseech of you that you will concur with M:M: [Madame May] and myself, so that we may see very soon the end of this affair. I will not conceal from you that it appears to me that Mr d'Hervart endeavours to differ it, and he finds some pretext for that; but as my life and happiness depends entirely upon my union with M:M: I declare, my dear father, most sincerely and upon my honour, that I cannot determine myself of ever leaving her a moment. Therefore, I hope you will find, as myself, that it is time to finish. I take the liberty of opening myself to you as to an intimate friend, by laying before you my miserable unhappy situation.

This 'miserable unhappy situation' referred to the fact that a marriage settlement had still not been agreed and Rowland was worried that his intended's father, Mr d'Hervart, was about to come up with a reason to kybosh the plans. Becoming desperate, Rowland begged his father to send a marriage contract containing terms that would keep d'Hervart happy.

so that I may present it to him, and hope that you will do everything that lays in your possession to induce him to a speedy conclusion … for I cannot think of staying any longer absent from you; it is useless depending on Mr d'Hervart's departure on account of his uncertainties, and on the other hand I can never determine myself of leaving this lady.

Leaving Switzerland with Sabine on his arm was the one thing that Rowland declared would 'entirely complete' his happiness. And with a contract in place, all that was left for the eager Rowland to do was to seek his father's blessing, 'which I hope you will be so good as to grant us, so that we may live entirely happy and content all the rest of our life.' Well, actually there were a few other things Rowland desired.

He asked his father to tell Mr d'Hervart that he approved of the match, and urged him *not* to let on that as soon as the marriage celebrations were over the couple planned to depart for England immediately. What a schemer young Rowland had become!

By November that year (1761), Rowland's father was in Paris, still brokering the marriage contract. Four of his daughters who still lived at home at Nostell, namely Susanna, Ann, Mary and Charlotte, wrote a letter to their 'Pappa' that month to tell him how much they were missing him. It had been four months since they had last seen him and they couldn't remember a time when they had been 'so long parted before'.

'Your goodness,' they wrote, 'in consenting to what my brother thinks will make his happiness complete, we hope he will always have gratitude to acknowledge, and as you seem to think he is sensible of his own misconduct, we flatter ourselves that is one step towards amendment and that his future behaviour will (in some degree) atone for the trouble he has given you.' The girls were anxious to know all about their brother's bride, 'but if her person is not any way remarkable, she will certainly appear to the greater advantage than she would have done had we heard more about her.' And they worried, like their father, that the language barrier would prove a real problem.

> We are afraid we shall be greatly at a loss to keep up a conversation with her, as you say she knows nothing of the English language and we have forgot the greatest part of our French. But supposing we had not, all the phrases are so very different that she would never understand us.

The letter is also worthy of note because the girls referred to a bridge that was currently under construction and still stands today at Nostell ('the workmen at the bridge go on fair and easily'). This structure was finished during the year they wrote the letter and in honour of its unveiling, the chief architect, Sir George Savile, wrote an epic poem, which ended:

> *Till Silver Went* [the river Went] *is plundered of its streams*
> *Till Sol forgets to warm us with his beams*
> *Till Nostel-Hall's laid level with the ground*
> *And not one stone upon another's found,*
> *Till Winn and Savile lose their very name*
> *Nostel, thy Bridge, shall stand enrolled in fame.*

The sisters ended their letter by wishing their father, brother and Sabine 'a safe voyage and good journey to Nostell (the sooner the better) and [we] hope our dear Pappa will ever believe us his dutiful daughters.'

And so it came to pass that on 4 December 1761, Rowland's tutor, Isaac Dulon, married the couple at St Claire's Protestant Church in Vevey. At twenty-seven it was time for the new Mrs Winn, who was the only surviving child of Philip and Jeanne Esther d'Hervart, to leave her homeland for a new life in England.

'Foulby Bridge', otherwise Nostell Bridge.

The marriage entry for Rowland Winn and Sabine Louise May.

411

1761

le 4º. Decembre 1761.

Wuin. Rowland Wuin, fils de Rowland Wuin, Cheval. Baronet, Anglois, et Sabine Louise May, née D'Herwart fille du Seigneur Baron, Iaques Philippe D'Herwart, de Vevey, ont été epousés dans le Temple de St. Claire Paroisse de Vevey, le Vendredy 4. Xbre 1761, à huit heures du Matin, par Isaac Dulon, Ministre du St. Evangile ensuitte d'un Brevet des Illustres Seigneurs du Supréme Consistoire du supréme Consistoire de Berne, en datte du 26. 9bre 1761.

The best part of six years would pass before the couple celebrated the birth of a first child, and in that time they'd enjoy visiting relatives, socializing in London and then, when Death came to claim the 59-year-old 4th Baronet on 23 August 1765, Sabine and the new 5th Baronet made Nostell their home.

Cousin Catherine

With the old man gone, this was the era of the 5th Baronet, and his peculiar wife, and not everybody was happy with the new order. The autobiography of a particularly miffed relative has survived and in a few scathing passages, the author made her feelings about the couple clear. The *Memoirs of the life of the late Mrs Catharine Cappe, written by herself* was published in 1822 in London and then in Boston, USA a year later.

Mrs Catherine Cappe (as her forename was more commonly written) who achieved renown as a writer and something of a do-gooder, was, in 1765, Miss Harrison, a 21-year-old relative of the Winns, Catherine's mother, Sarah, being a first cousin of the 4th Baronet. Following the death of Catherine's father, the Reverend Jeremiah Harrison, in July 1763, Catherine, then nineteen, was sent by her mother to live at Nostell with the Winns while her mother went to live with a brother in a cottage a few miles away. To say Catherine admired the 4th Baronet would be an understatement. In her memoirs she described visits to the house at Nostel (as she called it) prior to her move there, extolling the virtues of the head of the house.

> I had repeatedly made visits of some weeks at Nostel, and had always been well received there with the greatest kindness by the worthy proprietor, who had been the intimate friend of my father, as well as the near relation of my mother; I was also much attached to his three unmarried daughters, the oldest of whom presided as mistress of his family, and had particularly honoured me by her notice and friendship, notwithstanding she was nine years older than myself. I shall digress a little, in order to describe the hospitable style of ancient splendour, which prevailed in this friendly mansion, and at the same time, to pay a small tribute of affection and gratitude to the memory of one, who was generally and deservedly honoured and esteemed.

The 4th Baronet and his wife had six daughters in total who were: Susanna, who died unmarried in 1761; Elizabeth-Letitia, who married Sir George Strickland in 1751; Catherine, who married Nathaniel Cholmley in 1750; Ann, who married her father's second cousin, Sir George Allanson-Winn, in 1765; and Mary and Charlotte, who both died as spinsters. When she wrote of the 'mistress of the family', Catherine was referring to Ann Winn, prior to her marriage to Sir George. Ann was indeed nine years older than the author, being baptized at Wragby on 31 December 1734, whilst Catherine was born at Long Preston on 3 June 1744.

Writing about the 4th Baronet, Catherine described a man who had 'been a widower many years'. He was born in 1706 and was in his late fifties when she came to stay, and Catherine wrote that he lived in a manner 'not wholly dissimilar to that of an English baron, in ancient times'. She wrote of the respect her host commanded and the 'general happiness' that thrived.

Catherine described the scene that greeted a visitor to the 'splendid mansion', writing of an 'extensive park, approached by a long avenue of trees, and sheltered on the north-east by a wood of stately oaks, which had firmly withstood the winter blasts of successive centuries, [and] had all the grandeur, without the terrific gloom of the ancient Gothic castle'.

It was certainly a busy house during this period and Catherine was sure there were not less than 'sixty or seventy persons' working on the estate,

Catherine Cappe, from her autobiography.

who were often to be found dining in the servant's hall at mealtimes. Whilst documents in the Nostell archive record that the mansion was fully occupied by family and servants by the time of the 4th Baronet's death in 1765, it is possible that by 'servant's hall' she referred to the older building of the Gargrave era, though this would soon be torn down. Reading Catherine's memoirs, we even get a glimpse of what a Nostell Christmas was like. In her own words, without the merest hint of sardonicism, she tells us:

> it was at Christmas that the resemblance to the seat of the ancient baron was most striking. At this cheerful season, open house was kept for three days; all the farmers and cottagers upon the estate were invited along with their wives to dine in the great hall, precisely at two o'clock; where the worthy master of the whole family, (for they all appeared as his children,) presided at one long table with the men, and his amiable daughters at a second table with the women.

Having set the scene – no boy-girl-boy-girl seating at an eighteenth-century Nostell Christmas – Catherine went on to recall the food and entertainment on offer.

> The venerable boar's head, decorated with evergreens, and an orange in his mouth, according to the custom, was the centre dish at each table. A band of music played during dinner; after which the particular circumstances of every farmer and cottager, were carefully enquired into and many little plans formed for the alleviation or relief of their various anxieties or distresses. In the afternoon, some of the daughters of the most respectable farmers, were invited to partake of tea, coffee, cakes, and sweetmeats; and the evening concluded with a dance, in which they were permitted to join with the young ladies of the family and their other visitors, of whom there were several from Wakefield, Pontefract and the surrounding neighbourhood.

The daughters of the hoi polloi were permitted to stay until nine o'clock before they were shown the door. With the common folk out of the way, Catherine explained that the 'family and their guests adjourned into another apartment', where they tucked into a scrumptious supper. But the locals didn't go hungry, Catherine pointing out that, thrice weekly, meaty leftovers were sent out to a couple of nearby villages, along with a daily supply of milk. Reflecting on this time in her life, Catherine concluded that this was not a very useful act of charity; presumably she felt it was better that the villagers learned to be self-sufficient, but she remembered being greatly impressed by it at the time. She also recalled marvelling at how efficiently the estate was run with the 'orderly attendants, all arranged in their proper ranks'. But it was the 'appearance, character, manners, and occupations of the possessor himself … [which] supplied the finishing charm.'

Whilst Catherine obviously admired the 4th Baronet, she was also able, by extolling his virtues, to contrast his person with the 'vulgar' 5th Baronet. To ram home her estimations of the older man she went on to assert that he 'was singularly graceful, his countenance beamed with benevolence, and in his address, there was all the politeness, without the formality, of what is called the old school.'

In one of Catherine's now familiar digressions, she wrote a little of the young life of the 4th Baronet, describing how he'd been orphaned at a young age, his parents, another Sir Rowland, the 3rd Baronet and his wife Letitia both having died within seven days of each other in 1722 when the 4th Baronet was barely sixteen. The young lad was sent to live with his uncle, Edmund Winn, who was Catherine's maternal grandfather. From there he was packed off to Geneva to be educated and later, having returned to England, he stood for election. Though this bid ended in failure he did hold office as a magistrate.

Catherine was well acquainted with the daily routines of the 4th Baronet. She said he rose early, even on winter mornings, when he would 'kindle his own fire'. After this he'd spend time letter writing and then take his breakfast 'always exactly at nine o'clock'. Then at last Catherine tempered her hitherto universal praise for the man when she remarked that he wasn't 'possessed of shining talents, or eminent for literary attainments' but he was 'uniformly cheerful'. He spent some of his time visiting the Foundling Hospital at nearby Ackworth, which would later house Ackworth School, the famous Quaker school established in 1779. The hospital, an extension to Thomas Coram's Foundling Hospital in London, had not long been open by the time of Catherine's recollections.

It was his delight to visit these children, which he generally did two or three times in the week; examining their diet, inquiring into their health and respective improvements, and investigating the conduct of the matron, master, and other assistants.

This is all very well but perhaps the baronet, with all his influence, was too nice for his own, and the children's, good, for an account of the history of the school, published in 1853 as *A History of Ackworth School*, had this to say of the building's time as a hospital:

> benevolent as was the design, it was based on a fundamental error, and, as a natural consequence, it failed. Disease and death carried off great numbers annually; starvation, and even murder, on the part of nurses who had the care of the infants, and of masters to whom the elder children were apprenticed, added to the mortality; and though the evidence is abundant of the untiring efforts of the directors to care for the children whilst in the hospital, and to protect their rights after they were apprenticed, evils and oppressions, unnumbered and insurmountable, paralyzed their exertions, and the establishment was given up.

Surely, if conditions were so terrible, Catherine's messianic cousin would have done something about it rather than apparently turning a blind eye. Perhaps things weren't as bad as all that. Catherine wrote of the effect these hospital visits had on Sir Rowland, who'd got to know many of the children. She couldn't forget 'the animation and fine expression of his countenance, when, on his return, he delighted to detail the various little occurrences which had interested him, to an attentive and affectionate group of family auditors.'

But life at Nostell was destined to change and Catherine's 'gay delusion', as she described her life with her extended family, 'soon vanished'. The baronet's prodigal son and heir had returned, new wife in tow, and Catherine didn't like this one bit, telling her readers that the peace of the family was 'entirely destroyed' – and all while the 4th Baronet lay stricken on his couch with a perilous injury to his leg. 'The son was in every respect,' Catherine complained, 'the reverse of his father; but withal, elegant in his person and manner, specious in conversation, and insinuating in his address.' But it was the future Dame Sabine Louise Winn for whom Catherine reserved her harshest criticism and it's interesting that Christopher Todd wrote in the introduction to his 2005 paper that Sabine 'appears ... as a somewhat passive, self-centred figure who does not fit the model of the strong female chatelaine favoured in recent historiography.' Perhaps Todd's historiographers omitted to read, or ignored, Catherine Cappe's memoirs for her impression of Sabine was scathing: 'Trifling in her turn of mind and in her temper'; 'violent and imperious'; 'covetous and extravagant'. She did confess that she found her 'very beautiful', conceding that Sabine possessed a 'captivating' manner, and a 'great deal of vivacity', and admitted that she was somewhat awestruck when she first met her.

> When I first saw her, she was habited in a close vestment of pink satin, the colour not more delicate than her own fine complexion; she was tripping lightly along one of the great staircases; and seeing a stranger with one of the ladies of the family, ran up, and accosted us in French, with all the gaiety, ease, and politeness, peculiar to that nation; [though of course Sabine was Swiss] her fine dark eyes sparkling with a radiance exclusively their own.

In fact, Catherine was so stuck that she felt as if she had encountered an angel, but in looks only. She wrote that the younger Rowland would badmouth his father in front of all comers and had nothing pleasant to say about Ann, the sister of whom Catherine was so fond. This was because 'Nostel was not immediately resigned to him on his return from Switzerland the preceding year, and that his sister still occupied her seat at the head of the table.' To get his hands on the mansion Rowland would have to wait for his father's death. But with the older man confined to his bed, laid low by the injury he'd suffered, Rowland went out of his way to cause trouble, taking every opportunity to provoke his sister. His chosen method was to belittle her at mealtimes while in company. Ann bore the abuse, telling Catherine that 'this will be over when my father resumes his place; I could not resent it without a quarrel, and I would much rather endure anything than that he should have the pain of being made acquainted with my brother's unkind behaviour.'

Despite Catherine's frequent visits to Nostell she had never met the future 5th Baronet before. Upon their introduction Rowland resorted to his usual trick, belittling his sister. But, as Catherine put it, 'he had no real cause of complaint,' and she said this almost drove him mad, and made him hate her more. Catherine, not rising to the bait by joining him in abusing her friend, was also targeted by Rowland, who, now well into his twenties, was very immature. Apparently, he treated Catherine 'as one proscribed, and whom it was lawful to take every opportunity of insulting'. She says he blurted out double entendres, 'which it was impossible not to understand' and only gave up when his father was restored to his position at the table.

Later in her memoirs Catherine described Nostell's fortunes a whole year on. The baronet-in-waiting was in better spirits for he was about to see the back of his sister, Ann. She was soon to marry a long-standing acquaintance, Sir George Allanson-Winn of Little Warley in Essex, her distant cousin who'd inherited the estates of another cousin and who was a Baron of the Exchequer, and later a relatively unimpressive Member of Parliament for Ripon. Catherine had returned to Nostell at this time, the spring of 1765, presumably to attend the wedding, which took place at Wragby church on 12 April (and not in March as Catherine thought she remembered). She remained at Nostell until the July, and recorded that during this time Rowland and Sabine behaved very differently towards her, 'his lady', as Catherine called her, being particularly 'profuse in her expressions of esteem and friendship'. Maybe they sensed that there wouldn't be long left to wait before they got their hands on the biggest prize of all: Nostell itself.

That July, Catherine travelled to Boynton in the East Riding of Yorkshire to visit another of Rowland's sisters, Lady Elizabeth-Letitia Strickland and her husband, Sir George Strickland, with the other members of the Winn family set to join her there. But then disaster struck: 'on 22nd August,' Catherine wrote, '… a letter arrived with the mournful intelligence that Sir Rowland [the 4th Baronet] was very dangerously ill; and which was followed, in a few hours, by an express to desire Sir G. and Lady Strickland would set out immediately to Nostel.'

As quickly as a carriage could be readied, the party, Catherine included, set out at speed to journey to Nostell and the bedside of the 4th Baronet. Racing through the night, they reached the halfway point, the City of York, but on arriving there they were told of the baronet's death. The baronetcy immediately passed to his son and namesake. The *Leeds Intelligencer* and *Derby Mercury*, among others, reported the death in their newspapers on 27 August and 6 September, respectively:

> On Friday last died, of an inflammation in his Bowels, at his Seat in Nostel, near Pontefract, Sir Rowland Wynne, Bart.

> Last Saturday died, at his Seat at Nostall, near Pontefract, Sir Rowland Winn, Bart. He was many years in the Commission of the Peace for the West-Riding of this Country, and served the Office of Sheriff in 1732. He is succeeded in Title and Estate by his eldest Son, now Sir Rowland Winn.

The confusion over the date was probably down to the time of death. Catherine Cappe wrote that Sir Rowland had expired from a 'pestilential carbuncle, which was not understood by the surgeon who attended, and a

Plaque in Wragby church in memory of Sir Rowland Winn and his wife, Lady Susanna, and their daughter, Elizabeth.

mortification came on very rapidly.' It wasn't long before the baronet's last will and testament was proved and his estate distributed.

The baronet wrote his will on 27 April 1758, desiring his body be 'deposited in my family vault in Wragby church in as private a manner as possible.' This wish was carried out and an entry in the Wragby parish registers made on 3 September confirms he was 'interr'd in his Family Vault'. He was laid to rest with his wife, who had died over two decades earlier.

'And as to the worldly estate wherewith it hath pleased the almighty to bless me,' the baronet continued, 'I give and dispose of the same in manner and form following.' Firstly, as per his own marriage settlement, Sir Rowland gave all his 'manors, advowsons, messuages, land, tenements, and hereditaments in the county of York, Lincoln, and Cornwall' to his son, Rowland, 'and the heirs male of his body'. Of course, in 1758 young Rowland was unmarried and so just in case he shouldn't produce any male heirs, the same real estate would have gone to Rowland's brother, Edward, the 4th Baronet's second-born son, who was known as Neddy in his youth, and then to Edward's male heirs. And should Edward have fallen short in the male heir-producing department then the testator's brother, Edmund, would have scooped the jackpot (and so on until all possible male-line failures were accounted for). As it turned out, Sabine would give birth to a son, also named Rowland, in 1775 at the couple's London house, 11 St James's Square, which they'd recently purchased.

Once he'd finished ensuring a male Winn inherited his real estate the late baronet confirmed bequests of £1,300 on each of his daughters, Susanna Winn, Elizabeth-Letitia Strickland, Mary, Charlotte and Ann Winn (the will being written prior to her marriage in 1765), and to his granddaughters, Katherine and Mary Cholmley, daughters of the baronet's daughter, Catherine, he left £1,300 to share between them. The baronet appointed his son-in-law, Nathaniel Cholmley, his cousin, Thomas Winn of Acton, and future son-in-law, George Winn of Lincoln's Inn, as the executors of his will and also as guardians of those of his children who had not yet reached twenty-one. Each executor was given £100 for his troubles. And for good measure he left the residue of his personal estate to his eldest son, Rowland, should there have been any funds remaining after Rowland had discharged the monetary legacies to his siblings.

St James's Square in 1773, from Cassell's *Old and New London, volume four*.

Before he'd finally sealed his will, the 4th Baronet drew up a codicil on 10 March 1762 whereby he instructed his son, Rowland, to pay Hannah Rownsly, the 4th Baronet's housekeeper, an annuity of £30. He also willed that £400 be raised to pay to Hannah's daughter, 'commonly called Hannah Richardson', when she reached twenty-one, or on the day of her marriage, if that came sooner. Clearly the baronet thought highly of his staff, who were expected to work hard, as shown in an undated document entitled *Business expected to be done by the porter at Nostell*. This shows that the porter was charged with plenty of responsibility, detailed in fourteen points in the following instructions:

1. To clean the low dineing room, passage, Low Hall, Stewards Room, Servants Hall, and passage to the Kitching every day.
2. To make fires in the Low Rooms when occation.
3. To wait at the Stewards Room Table, to Clean the Knives, Lay the cloth &c.
4. To light the lamps in the passage.
5. To cutt the Wood for the Ovans when wanted.
6. To see that all the Doors and Windows are made fast at night and opened in the morning.
7. To go up once a week to see that the Gutters in the Roof of the House be clean that there be no dirt in them to stop [document damaged here].
8. To Sweep out the Roof of the House … from Dust &c.
9. To help get Coals into the cellar.
10. To help the Housekeeper in Spring to Distill Herbs.
11. To seek yeast when wanted for Bakeing.
12. Not to give away any Victuals or Drink out of the House unless by particular orders.
13. Not to permit any strangers to be Loytering in the Servants Hall but to enquire whom they want and then to see for that person and to be able to give me or any of the Upper Servants an account who they are and what they want and if they cannot give some account of themselves to turn them out and to complain to me or to Allen or to the Butler who shall first be met.
14. To help clean the sashes when wanted or other trifleing jobs about the House.

Allen is a reference to Henry Allen, who worked at Nostell during the eighteenth century and witnessed the 4th Baronet's will in 1758 (in which same year he married at Wragby Church).

An illustration of who sat at the servants' table at this time is contained within the Nostell archive, titled *Liste de L'arangement des place a la table de la Servants Hall*, and is recreated below showing the various roles employed at the house. The French title gives away the fact that it dates from Lady Sabine Winn's time.

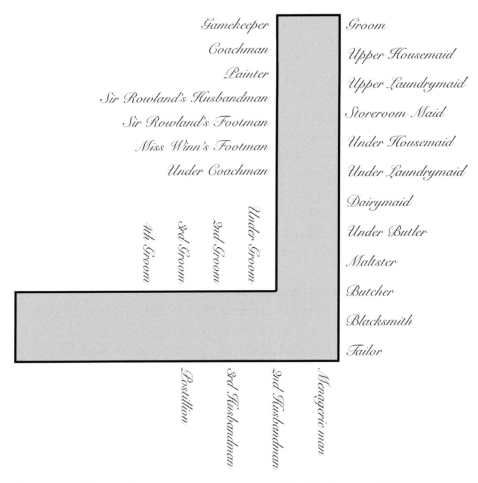

Recreation of *Liste de L'argangement des place a la table de la Servants Hall*.

A new era at Nostell

Whilst the new baronet and his wife would make changes to the house on such a grandiose scale that they would almost bring the family to financial ruin, they didn't immediately move in, instead remaining, for a time, in a house a few miles away at Badsworth, which they had borrowed from the Marquess of Rockingham, a family friend and future prime minister.

For the final time, candid insight into the characters of the 5th Baronet and his wife Sabine is provided by the ever frank Catherine Cappe, whom Sabine had invited to Badsworth to stay. Sabine wanted Catherine present when she and the baronet were paying calls at neighbouring houses owing to Sabine's 'imperfect knowledge of the English', which, Sabine worried, would 'make her much at a loss'.

Things went well for the first few weeks as the trio paid calls at the homes of all the right people, though Catherine was alarmed by the 'irregular' hours kept by the couple, who were so lazy as to not sit down for breakfast until 'twelve or one', and didn't dine until 'seven or eight'. But what shocked her most was the way the couple treated an old lady whom they'd also invited to stay with them. Catherine explained that the lady was not blessed with great judgement and had in her youth been considered quite a beauty, and was thus somewhat vain and eager to please the couple. Apparently the new baronet possessed an odd-sounding 'electrical machine' with which he carried out 'experiments' and the poor elderly house guest was 'frequently the subject'. The baronet also had an air pump into which he put small creatures, such as mice, to examine the effects of depriving them of oxygen. He knew the old dear detested mice, and playing on her fears he repeated threats to set them loose. When she wasn't being terrorized by the promise of having rodents run about her feet, Sabine was forcing the woman to stay up until the early hours of the morning, which, Catherine tells us, was ultimately 'ruinous to her health'. She decided to challenge Lady Winn about this and received the following reply: 'I keep her out of charity, and have a right to expect that she should conform to my pleasure.'

It seems Catherine wasn't the couple's first choice as interpreter, for prior to her arrival, Rowland and Sabine had entertained the daughter of a local yeoman. Sabine had apparently showered the girl with trinkets, which she'd insisted the girl wore to the point that she ended up looking completely out of place and became a figure of ridicule in the house. During Catherine's stay she heard the girl, who had since left the Winn's company, being continually mocked. Again she challenged the mistress, asking why she'd resorted to making the girl look so daft. Catherine wrote that the reply came in broken English and was honest, if nothing else. 'My dear, I tell you one truth, I do it express for the ridicule.' This was too much for poor Catherine:

> 'If that, madam, be the construction which your ladyship's young friends are to put upon your favours, they would be abundantly better without them,' relinquishing at the same moment, her arm on which I had leaned, as we were walking backwards and forward in the dining-room. She appeared confused, was profuse in her professions of regard to me, declaring that the like with respect to myself could never happen; but from that moment, we perfectly understood each other, (for she was not deficient in acuteness of perception) and my determination was fixed, to leave the family as soon as I could do it, with decency and propriety; and it so happened, that what I had resolved upon as a matter choice and of duty, became afterwards a matter of absolute necessity.

Catherine had a brother who at this time was a student at the University of Cambridge. Perhaps to placate her, he had been invited to Badsworth. He accepted and the siblings were duly reunited. When Catherine had begun her stay at Nostell, back in 1763, the late baronet had assured her that he was going to do whatever he could to help her brother, who was then new to university life, but for whom a career in the Church was intended. Sir Rowland wrote to the Archbishop of York, a friend of his, requesting advice on the best course of study for the young man, and a helpful reply was received. For this Catherine remained grateful, and she was obviously protective of her sibling.

During the visit the new baronet had become sullen and moody, puncturing long silences with 'incidental flashes of sarcasm'. Catherine could tell this tension was building to something darker and she waited for the storm to hit. One night an incident occurred that could have come straight from an episode of *Downton Abbey*.

The baronet had invited some guests, who were, to put it one way, some rungs beneath him on the eighteenth-century social ladder. After dinner they assembled in one of the drawing rooms. Suddenly, Catherine heard her brother's voice calling out so she went to find out what was going on. She was met by the baronet, who told her that her brother was drunk, so drunk, in fact, that a 'fit of delirium' had been brought on. But, he insisted, she wasn't to worry for he and the others in his company were going to carry him off to bed.

Catherine wasn't buying this. She was convinced that the baronet had added 'some drug of an intoxicating quality' to the liquor. When things had calmed down she went once more to see the baronet, and tiring of the pretence she made her suspicions known. To try to convince her that this wasn't the case, the baronet told her that her brother was well known at Cambridge for his drunkenness. That was the final straw:

'Strange, sir, if that had really been the case, that I should never have heard the least intimation of it; besides, surely at your own table you might have checked the propensity before it produced such terrible effects. We shall leave your house, sir, tomorrow morning.'

And so they did, apparently leaving Sabine in floods of tears as Catherine and her brother walked out of the door, never to see Lady Winn again. Seven years later, she did find herself in the company of the 5th Baronet, who was staying at his sister's home in Boynton. 'He expressed himself,' Catherine began, 'with a sort of ironical politeness, as being glad to see me; and afterwards, in a long conversation, seriously protested … that he was the most unhappy man alive – that he had not a friend in the world.' So it seemed that getting his hands on all his heart's desires did not equate to perpetual happiness.

One of Sir Rowland's first acts upon entering his family seat was to replace the architect James Paine. Paine had executed now famous designs at Nostell, which include the decorative ceilings in the dining room and state bedroom. In Paine's place Sir Rowland hired Robert Adam and his brother James to complete the unfinished building work. Sir Rowland also engaged Antonio Zucchi, a neoclassical painter, the plasterer Joseph Rose (whose uncle, also Joseph Rose, had worked at Nostell with James Paine), and famously, Thomas Chippendale, the furniture maker, as the 5th Baronet strove to realize his vision for Nostell. Or perhaps he was engaging in a spot of one-upmanship to ensure he stepped out of the shadow cast by the legacy of his universally popular dead father. In his 1915 work on Nostell, Maurice Brockwell wrote:

> Vast as the house is, it was not considered large enough for the fancy of Sir Rowland, the 5th Baronet, who succeeded his father in 1765. For him Robert Adam made designs for four new wings, of which only one was finished. A very considerable amount of interior decoration was planned and carried to completion by Adam, under whose direction Joseph Rose did a large amount of 'Plaisterers Work' between 1766 and 1777.

Sir Rowland didn't waste any time in beginning work on Nostell, as a letter from Joseph Rose testifies. The baronet had written to the plasterer, who was based in London, and Rose's reply, dated 7 November 1765, just weeks after the death of the 4th Baronet, discussed meeting to finalize work at Nostell.

> if you have any thoughts of being here any part of this winter Sir, & was to bring with you the sections of the Hall & Saloon the finishings would be most conveniently settled here; they are fine rooms & I make no doubt but you will finish them as they deserve; if you do not come to Town this winter, I shall be very happy in doing anything in my power relative to the above business; & in the spring I shall be in Yorkshire again when I hope to have the honour to wait on you at Nostell.

In another letter, dated 16 August 1766, Zucchi the painter wrote of 'drawings for the Hall', which he said were to be 'executed in Basso-rivelo'. He included in his letter annotated 'plans for the saloon', which Adam had drawn up, marking where pictures were to be placed. In this letter there are hints that Zucchi was nervous about receiving payment for his work, which he suggested he was offering at the lowest possible price, and indeed the 5th Baronet would gain a reputation as a bad payer of his bills.

> I remitted to Mr Adams the whole account for all the work I have done for you, on which I have set the nearest price, such that I never have, nor could

I for any other Gentleman, make an account with so much restriction, however I gave to Mr Adams [sic] the faculty to arbitrate to settle with you, well knowing that both are connoisseurs and respectable enough.

Brockwell suggested that Zucchi was 'always eager for extremely prompt payment' and had actually priced his paintings too highly, his opinion of himself being even higher, but given the number of tradesmen who chased the 5th Baronet for payment, Zucchi was probably making sure he didn't end up out of pocket.

Adam himself wrote to Sir Rowland requesting that certain sums of money be paid on account, such as the £100 he asked for in 1767 in a letter that contained a request for the same sum to be paid on Zucchi's account. Brockwell seemed surprised that Zucchi should request regular payment for his work, and there was another such application via a letter from Adam sent to Sir Rowland a month later. This read, 'As he has now done a good deal of work upon these, you are no doubt perfectly safe to advance him the difference, but I would have you do in this whatever is most agreeable to yourself,' whilst assuring the baronet he'd make sure Zucchi provided a receipt.

Brockwell illustrated just how quickly work had advanced by the careful choice of the letters he cited from the Nostell archive. He included a letter from Benjamin Ware, a servant at Nostell, dated 1770 in which Ware gave the baronet a progress report on the building work. Ware wrote (not very skilfully) that Rose had completed a frame around the ceiling in the saloon, that the joiners had completed work in the saloon, save for some doors, and that the 'gardners Lodgin Room and s'rnt [servants'] Room has Been finisht some time,' going on to explain that the Lower Room 'will be finisht verey soun.'

By this time Sir Rowland and Lady Sabine had become parents, their daughter Esther Sabina Winn being born in 1768 at 11 St James's Square in London, the town house that Sir Rowland had bought two years earlier. As at Nostell, Robert Adam, along with his brothers, would also carry out extensive work on this house in the years to come, paid for from the ever diminishing Nostell coffers.

In the same year as Ware's letter was written, a Mr J. Blackburn, a tradesman of Carey Street, London, wrote to Sir Rowland requesting payment of yet another unpaid bill. This was the beginning of a saga where letters flew back and forth, and Blackburn even sent one to Henry Allen in which he wrote that the word of Sir Rowland was worthless and 'not to be depended on', which did not go down well when Sir Rowland got to hear about it!

In August 1777, Rose the plasterer, who had drawn up and sent detailed accounts to Sir Rowland (which ran to forty-nine pages and covered *Plasisters Work done at his House at Nostell, From the year 1766 to 1777 Under the Direction of Messrs Robert and James Adam, Architects*), wrote to Robert Adam to complain that his account for work at Nostell had not been settled satisfactorily and that unfair deductions had been made. He pointed out that he'd actually undercharged Sir Rowland:

> I also beg leave to mention another circumstance which may possibly have escaped your attention, viz. that I have not made the customary charge for the men travelling to & from Nostel during the course of eleven years which that work has been in hand, nor any charge made for the carriage of their boxes; nor even the Packing cases for the medallions & models sent from London, nor Porterage for anything. The truth is (& ashamed I am to say it) that a regular account has not been kept of these things; and as I could not make an accurate account I have made none at all; & however moderate I meant to be in my charge to Sir Rowland Winn, I think some allowance for these things should be made in my favour, after having offered these things to your consideration, I have only to add the whole is finally submitted to your determination.

In his letters to the baronet, Robert Adam described himself as Sir Rowland's 'Most sincere humble servant', and often ended his letters affectionately, such as in 1776 when he begged 'to be remembered to Lady Winn & yourself in the most warm manner wishing the young ones a continuation of that excellent health & spirits they enjoyed when I left you.' He sent Sir Rowland a letter dated 5 September 1777, with which he enclosed Rose's note. In his letter he told the baronet that his accountant, Mr Wallace, had been through Rose's accounts with a fine toothcomb and noted Rose's dissatisfaction. Adam also pointed out that Rose had given his consent for the Adam brothers to settle the account. However, Adam conceded that as the work had been carried out over such a long time, 'there is no help for it.' 'It is a pity,' Adam continued, 'you had not settled sooner with him, that the state of accounts might have been known, which are always most distinct when kept short.' Rose was ultimately cheered when the baronet settled his account to his liking, commenting in a letter dated 1 September 1778 that settlement had 'one year's interest add to it (in consideration of its not being paid sooner)'.

Chippendale at Nostell

Even the great Thomas Chippendale, the celebrated furniture maker who was born at Otley, near Leeds in 1718, had cause for complaint. He'd begun work, under Robert Adam's instruction, on the first of many pieces that he made for Nostell Priory by at least 21 June 1766, as shown in Chippendale's detailed account book, which survives in the Nostell archives. On 24 June 1766, an early entry in the account book refers to 'a very large mahogany book case with glass doors and a pediment top' for which Chippendale charged £38, and on 30 June the following year there is an entry for the elegant desk that is still to be found in the Library, which was described in the account book as:

> a large mahogany Library Table of very fine wood, with doors on each side of the bottom part and drawers within on one side and partitions on the other, with terms to ditto carved and ornamented with Lion's head and paws, with carved ovals in the panels of the doors, and the top covered with black leather, and the whole completely finished in most elegant taste

Chippendale charged £72 10s 0d for this piece and it is justifiably described as one of his masterpieces, remaining on show today to visitors to the house. In fact, all of the Library furniture described in the account book in entries made from 1766 to 1768 can still be found in the Library at Nostell. But for all that Nostell was a prestigious contract, Chippendale, who had also received commissions from Sir Edwin Lascelles at Harewood House and the monarchy, was forced to write to Sir Rowland to chase payment, like any other tradesman in the employ of the baronet. Chippendale's account book shows that the work carried out for Nostell was costed in excess of £1,500, so it's perhaps unsurprising that slow payment couldn't be tolerated by an

Old postcard showing Chippendale's desk in the Library.

overworked artisan with his own bills to pay. Lindsay Boynton and Nicholas Goodison in their article for the journal *Furniture History* (volume 4, 1968) discussed the matter.

> Like many contemporary patrons he [Winn] was bad at paying bills, suffering perhaps from the lack of liquid funds common to eighteenth-century landowners, and thus he aggravated Chippendale's own cash problems. Unlike the patron, who could confidently take his time in paying his debts to tradesmen, Chippendale had to pay his journeymen weekly and settle his own bills every six or twelve months or pay interest on the amount due.

Sadly for Chippendale, Sir Rowland held all the aces, and as Boynton and Goodison pointed out, Chippendale, who was often paid in post-dated bank notes that duly bounced, did not always provide Sir Rowland with accounts when asked for them, nor indeed did he deliver furniture on time. In letters in the Nostell archive, Chippendale's excuses for his tardiness included being engaged on other 'large' jobs, having too much work to do, 'mostly for the Royal Family', and even, on one occasion, because he was suffering from a sore throat. This was too much for Sir Rowland who, in a letter of his own, dated 27 September 1767, decided to let Chippendale know precisely how he felt about him.

As your behaviour convinces me that do you not think my custom and protection worth paying any regard to, I shall endeavour to find out some other person that will be more grateful and that will not use me in the manner you have done which I shall not easily forget and must now tell you that you may expect to find me as great an enemy as I ever was your friend. It is not to be conceived the great expense and inconvenience you have put me to by your neglect therefore as I will not be trifled with any longer [I] desire you will send me my bill immediately, also the damask beds and glasses with the borders, finished or not. As the other furniture that you was to have made me, if they are not finished on the receipt of this letter you need not send them as I [will] get them elsewhere, the time being long expired that you promised to send them and that you declared if they did not come to the time you would not have one farthing for them, your behaviour to me is not to be bore & [I] shall take care to acquaint those gentleman that I have recommended you to and desire that they will oblige me in employing some other person.

Judging by Chippendale's next letter, he'd been firmly put in his place. It was dated 1 October 1767 and in it he acknowledged Sir Rowland's and made his apologies, said he'd 'taken it into his head' to think of the baronet as his patron, and hoped that all was not lost. He then tried to explain away the delays, referring to a dyer hired to work on the damask beds mentioned by Sir Rowland who had let him down, and that so much work was being carried out in London that it was impossible to 'get anything done'. He listed all the items he had completed, and the ones that were close to completion, and then finished by writing: 'I have nothing more to add but to hope for pardon and am in hopes that you will forgive me as I have done all that lay in my power.' Whilst this helped to heal the rift and Chippendale continued to work for Sir Rowland, their relationship was a strained one. Later that month Chippendale wrote again. This time he told the baronet that because he was such a bad payer he was now no longer able to get credit from Sir George Colebrooke, a merchant banker in London who had told Chippendale that Sir Rowland had the means to obtain a banker's draft at Wakefield at any time to the value of any sum of his liking. Then in January the following year, Chippendale wrote again to plead with the baronet for some cold hard cash.

> I have one favour to beg of your Honour, though I am really ashamed to ask one, which is if you could spare me a little cash it would be of the greatest service imaginable at this time as I have many large accounts to settle and money runs very short. I need not good Sir! explain myself any further as you know my necessity.

But evidently all that Sir Rowland could do was find fault. Chippendale's next note began with an apology to the baronet who was 'displeased' about a frame Chippendale had made for a barometer. This time Chippendale told Sir Rowland that the reason his work was so poor was because his foreman's wife had died a year earlier, followed by the death of the unlucky foreman's brother. More letters followed containing requests for money. And then in 1770, Chippendale wrote: 'I am very sorry that I am obliged to trouble you about the hundred pound note which you gave me.' Evidently, a remittance sent by the baronet had been refused, meaning Chippendale could not pay money he owed to the executors of his deceased business partner. Consequently, he was worried he would be arrested and he begged Sir Rowland not to 'let that happen to me'.

And so this went on, Sir Rowland replying to one such letter to say, 'do you think that I will pay such large sums and receive nothing for 'em and be content to be always disappointed.' The baronet repeated threats he'd made in a previous letter, telling Chippendale that 'if you do not know how to value a friend's protection you shall know the loss of one.'

If that wasn't sign enough of Sir Rowland's displeasure, he also added that he would have to return a commode that Chippendale had made for Dame Sabine, 'as it is too large.' This seemed to frustrate Chippendale who, in a letter dated 20 November 1770, told Sir Rowland that the baronet jolly well 'knew something of my situation after the death of my partner: I had but very little money to begin the world again which I told you,' going on to explain that the efforts he'd put himself to keep his head above water 'has been very near fatal to me.'

By January 1772, the baronet had received a final bill for the work Chippendale had carried out, over a period of almost six years. But he had not settled it, having raised questions about the amount requested. The furniture maker was becoming exasperated. He had amassed debts of his own, apparently totalling £4,600, and so he picked up his pen once more to tell Sir Rowland that it was time to pay up.

> The time for paying my money is now due, I have depended on your assisting me, nor can I tell what to do. Unless you assist me with the sum I requested of you I shall be utterly ruined. I humbly beg you will do all in your power to grant my request. You will please to observe in your account that most of the work has been done since the years 1767 and 68 and credit is too long for any man to support. I myself am obliged to pay my bills every twelve months and some at six months and if I over run the time I am obliged to pay interest.

The baronet duly sent a series of payments (after receiving at least one letter on the matter from a firm of London solicitors), but these did not satisfy the amount owed and Chippendale ultimately went to his grave, in November 1779, having never seen his accounts fully settled. That said, Chippendale's son and namesake carried on the family business and continued to take commissions from Nostell.

A comprehensive list of all the work Thomas Chippendale senior carried out for the 5th Baronet from June 1766 to June 1772 can be found in the account book described above, and a transcription features in the paper by Boynton and Goodison. It's certainly extremely detailed, and containing an inventory of all of the pieces he made for Nostell, as well as entries covering repairs and amendments, it offers as complete a picture of Chippendale's work there as any extant source, even down to nails, wood and tacks, which, on 23 April 1770, he gave to a man 'doing sundry jobs at your house'.

What it doesn't mention is the famous Nostell Dolls' House, the decorative model on show at Nostell depicting a typical, though stunning, early to mid-eighteenth-century country house that has been attributed to Chippendale by 'family tradition'. This attribution, given that the official guidebooks date the dolls' house to between 1730 and 1740, is not credible. Chippendale was barely a teenager in the earliest of those years, and the latest possible year, 1740, was twenty-six years before there is any documentary evidence of him first producing work for Nostell.

Whilst the authors of the various editions of the Nostell Priory guidebooks acknowledge 'there is no real evidence' for it, the Chippendale claim was repeated in a 2012 *Yorkshire Evening Post* newspaper article, which reported that the dolls' house was undergoing delicate cleaning work that spring. In this article, the writer specifically dated the dolls' house to 1735 (when Chippendale was just seventeen), the journalist stating: 'It was reputedly built by master craftsman Thomas Chippendale.' A staff member at Nostell Priory was quoted in the article as confirming this 'tradition', contrary to what appears in the guide on sale there, but added, 'Whilst we can't prove this, Nostell is home to one of the largest collections of Chippendale furniture in the country and the doll's [*sic*] house has many replica pieces of similar furniture in miniature.'

It seems the basis for the claim is that Chippendale was born in Otley and so must have used his Yorkshire 'connections' to find work at Nostell in his youth. And there is a similar tradition to explain how he came to obtain commissions at Harewood House. These 'traditions' were debunked by Christopher Gilbert in his 1978 epic *The Life and Work of Thomas Chippendale*, and by Kathleen Harris in her *Chippendale*, which was published in 1989, but the dolls' house claim endures in spite of this. Perhaps the thinking behind it is more to do with maintaining visitor numbers than upholding historical accuracy. Gilbert explained that in 1923, a descendant of a half-brother of Chippendale had 'disclosed that, according to inherited tradition, the Lascelles family of Harewood were responsible for promoting his famous ancestor's career.' But as Gilbert pointed out, these revelations had only been made after Chippendale's Otley origins had come to light – indeed, Brockwell thought that he'd been born in Wiltshire. Gilbert described the idea that Chippendale had worked at Nostell as a young man as a 'frivolous notion', although he conceded, as is well known, that there are 'lost years' in Chippendale's early life. He wrote, 'is it historically possible that he was employed in building the mansion under the direction of the youthful James Paine, who later subscribed to the *Director*?' This was Chippendale's well-known book, which was published in 1754, containing designs that attracted many of his subsequent commissions. Alluding to a paragraph in the 1968 Boynton and Goodison paper, Gilbert said that it had 'recently' been suggested that some of the letters written to Sir Rowland Winn 'hint at the existence of personal goodwill and previous contacts.' The letters in question were those where Winn threatened to call a halt to Chippendale's Nostell commission and Chippendale wrote to say he would be sorry to lose his 'patron'.

Gilbert dismissed the idea that Chippendale had undertaken a stint of employment at Nostell in his youth, pointing out that he was treated 'as an ordinary tradesman', rather than a family friend, and that the theory was 'worth recording' but was 'unconvincing'.

If we accept that a pre-pubescent Chippendale probably didn't pop to Nostell to knock up this astonishing model then we may also have to accept that he didn't put it together as an adult either. There is no mention of the dolls' house in any of the many letters flying back and forth between Chippendale and the 5th Baronet. Nor is there one single concrete allusion to an earlier association that a younger Chippendale had with Nostell or the family.

Whilst there may well be miniature copies of Chippendale pieces within the dolls' house, he could have added these later when he was working for the Winn family. Though if he did, he didn't make any charge for the work. And on the evidence cited above documenting the money issues that he had suffered at the hands of the slow-paying baronet, this is also unlikely, not least because Chippendale included every last nail and tack in his accounts.

Maybe the dating is wrong. If not, then more realistically, this beautiful, intricate model with its chinoiserie interiors, was executed for the 4th Baronet and his wife at the very time when that baronet commissioned early designs for the house itself, and possibly the model was built to a design by James Paine, for the exterior is certainly Palladian, just like Nostell. Or there could be another explanation. Maurice Brockwell, the art historian who wrote in such detail about the contents of Nostell Priory, had this to say (the italics are mine but the punctuation is his):

> The Doll's House is for convenience placed on the lower landing of this [the south] staircase. The generous scale on which it is designed may be best indicated by the fact that it measures 81 by 76 in., which the front door is 12 by 6¼ in. It was made about *1740* by the estate carpenter under the direction of *Lady Winn* and her sister *Miss Henshaw, who designed the scheme of decoration and carried out the innumerable details which its complete furnishing required.* The architecture and furniture of a doll's house always correspond with the prevailing taste of the day which produced them, and there can be no doubt that the general appearance and architectural features of Nostell Priory were adopted by the carpenter for the exterior of his doll's house.

Whoever built it, it is well worth a look.

Sir Rowland upsets the family

It wasn't just contractors who had to chase Sir Rowland for monies they were due. The baronet even avoided paying his siblings their shares of their late father's fortune, often ignoring letters requesting their dues.

An intriguing letter from Sir George Strickland, husband of Sir Rowland's sister, Lady Strickland of Boynton, suggested that letters they'd tried to send to Lady Sabine were being intercepted and kept from her. And worse, that somebody was answering on her behalf, without her knowledge. The culprit was presumed by the Stricklands to be Sir Rowland himself (who had upset the Stricklands by withholding money owed to Lady Strickland as per the terms of the will of their father, the 4th Baronet). Sir George feared that Sabine was being coached to 'avoid your real friends'. In the letter Sir George referred to the issue of the owed money and wrote of instructing his attorney to deal with Sir Rowland, but assured Sabine that she had no enemies at Boynton. One letter read:

Boyton 17 Oct: 1780

Madam

By the last post I received a letter dated from Nostell and signed S. Winn but in a hand so totally different from a former letter of your Ladyship's that I was in doubt whether to direct an answer to you or not. However, I have ventured to do it rather than hazard of being remiss in any respect that is due to your Ladyship, as this family have always been anxious and will ever continue desirous to merit your good opinion, but I am much afraid that you have been taught to avoid your real friends and from whom only you will ever hear the truth. After what I have said above I need hardly add that I have great doubt whether this letter will ever reach your hands, but should it not it will certainly fall in those of Sir Rowland Winn. I have only to add in regard to the business mentioned in the letter that if he means to pay the money at the time he has appointed, it can be no inconvenience to him or to your Ladyship for him to give me a security for doing therefore if he refuses it. I shall look upon his promise as only given to gain time and without any intent to pay me, as he has already frequently promised me the payment without ever keeping to his word. I shall therefore, unless he consents to my proposal by the return of the post, suffer my attorney to proceed, and I am certain did you know what manner I have been used by him that you would not only think that you have no enemy at Boynton but that I have forbore myself justice much longer than was reasonable. And I can't help thinking but that he has prejudiced you against Lady Strickland and prevents your seeing her, least you should hear such truths as would be grating to his ear to have repeated to him.

I am your Ladyship's sincere friend and honourable servant G Strickland

Six months later, Sir George wrote a letter to Sir Rowland, and his mood had not cooled. 'Had I not already waited fifteen years in order to oblige you and in dependence upon your promises, all of which you broke to me,' he began, 'you might have asked me to defer the payment of your money, as you now do, to an unlimited day.' Clearly Sir Rowland was still withholding the pennies, and in a letter he received in 1774 from his sister, Mary, she quoted him on the matter. Mary wrote that he'd said: 'you say we are a set of people who call ourselves your relations, who are always pestering you for money.' She added:

> I can answer that I never demanded or received from you anything but what was my due, and don't look on that as any indulgence, as you term it, and as we are the offspring of the same parents, it will not be a very easy matter to shake off the relationship, however desirous you may be of it. And am sure no one action of my life has ever been such that any relation I have, need wish to disown me and can't accuse myself of ever distrusting you in any respect, so you do me injustice to lay it to my charge.

Sir Rowland's sister Charlotte (a spinster, like Mary) also had cause to write to him several times chasing payments, and, like other relations, to admonish him for not replying to letters, but despite this, his siblings still desired the friendship of Sabine. Charlotte sent her brother a letter in 1768 congratulating him on the birth of his daughter, Esther, in which she asked how Sabine was and offered to wait upon her, 'as I fancy she has nobody with her at present, but don't mean to do it if it is any way disagreeable to you.'

The rogue election
When he wasn't busy threatening his contractors or withholding money from his siblings, the 5th Baronet was trying to grab a seat in Parliament, and his ultimate failure to do so might explain the melancholic state in which Catherine Cappe found him upon their last meeting.

In Sir Rowland's day, the parliamentary constituency of nearby Pontefract was a 'burgage borough', a burgage being a plot of land within a borough. There were 325 of these plots in Pontefract and whilst they were owned by several landowners, there were two who dominated the scene. Forty plots were held by the 5th Baronet, but Lord Galway held about double that number, and by 1766, John Walsh had around seventy-five, which he had purchased from the heir of the previous owner, George Morton Pitt. Between them, Galway and Walsh held another twenty-two plots. The rest were in the ownership of individuals who possessed one or two apiece.

At elections it was the burgesses who held the right to vote, with Pontefract returning two Members to Parliament. The rules allowed only one vote per person, so burgesses who held multiple plots could temporarily convey their remaining holdings to self-interested nominees, who could be relied upon to vote for the *right* man. Effectively, Galway and Walsh could choose their own candidates, ensuring they always won the day. That said, in previous years, rather than exerting their dominance, Lord Galway and Pitt had always made sure they consulted the other independent burgesses to ensure no ill will, and therefore avoided implementing what were known as faggot voters. But all this changed in 1767 when a new plan was hatched.

Walsh, the new burgage owner, convinced Lord Galway that they no longer needed to consult the other burgesses, who tended to live within the borough itself, and should certainly avoid talking to the non-voting plebs, whose opinions were of no interest to them. Instead, Walsh and Galway would now put up their own candidates without consulting anybody and thus fill the borough with faggot voters, come what may.

At the election of 1768, held on 21 March, these candidates would be Galway himself and Henry Strachey of Bristol, who was Walsh's man. Naturally, the independent burgesses were somewhat insulted and conspired to present a candidate of their own – none other than the 5th Baronet himself, who selflessly offered to stand. And he was a man with a plan.

When election day finally came, with the faggot voters duly installed, Sir Rowland knew his only hope of victory was to convince the ordinary folk of Pontefract to lend their muscle to dissuade these incomers from voting at all. And they didn't disappoint. The atmosphere in the town had already reached fever pitch, as the *Leeds Intelligencer* explained in their edition of 22 March 1768.

We hear from Pontefract that, Sir Rowland Wynn [*sic*], Bart having last week offer'd himself as a Candidate for that Borough, in opposition to Walsh, Esq; one of the old members, open houses are to be kept by both parties on the occasion; and the whole town is already a scene of tumult, riot, and confusion; the windows of several gentlemen's houses having been entirely broke to pieces by the outrageous mobs.

When the votes were finally counted, the Mayor of Pontefract announced that Lord Galway had been returned, having polled forty-four votes, along with Sir Rowland, who'd received forty-two. The baronet had succeeded where his father had failed – he was now a Member of Parliament. Strachey came in last place, having only received twenty-one votes. But with so many burgesses eligible to vote, why were these numbers so low? Did the 'atmosphere' described above have something to do with it? It sure did.

A letter dated a day after the election was sent to several provincial newspapers alleging a series of events that cast serious doubt on the legitimacy of the baronet's triumph. One of these newspapers was the *Public Advertiser*, which printed the letter in their 26 March 1768 edition.

> Yesterday began the Election at this Place, and I believe such a Scene of Riot and Confusion was never beheld at any other Election. In the Morning a very numerous Mob of Bargemen, &c. assembled from the neighbouring Towns, and marched into Pontefract with Colours flying, which they planted at the Door of the Town-Hall. When any Person in the Interest of Sir R. W[inn] appeared, he was permitted to enter the Hall; but when any of the Friends of the two other Candidates appeared they were insulted, repulsed, and for the most part beat, and some very dangerously wounded. As the Poll proceeded, the Riot increased. A Gentleman of the Corporation having given his Vote for Lord G[alway] and Mr S[trachey] the Mob dispatched a Party to his House, who broke down the Doors and Windows, and the House would in all Probability have been entirely pulled down if a Servant had not resolutely opposed the Mob at the Door with Fire-Arms. Many Gentlemen who had polled were assaulted and knocked down; and the Voters for Lord G. and Mr S. were so intimidated, that most of them fled from the Town last Night, and those few who stayed were confined within Doors. The Riot was so great during the Poll, that the Mayor was obliged to adjourn for an Hour, when none but Sir R.W. and his Friends could venture out of Court. At the second Opening, the Riots grew worse and on closing the Poll of that Day at Five in the Evening, it was found impossible for any of the Friends of Lord G. and Mr S. to go home without the personal Protection of some Gentlemen in Sir R.W.'s Interest, who attended them to the Star Inn, and found great Difficulty in preventing

the most fatal Outrages. These and many other tumultuous Proceedings of a similar Nature, obliged Lord G. and Mr S. by Advice of their Council to demand, by Letter to the Mayor, an Adjournment of the Poll until the Peace of the Town could be established. But as it appeared this Morning, that the Mob were again come into the Town, and were again parading about with their Colours, and that even those Voters who had stayed in Town could not venture to go to the Court with Safety of their Lives, the two Candidates sent to the Mayor a formal Protest against this riotous Mode of Election, and demanded that Mr Mayor should close the Poll immediately, that the Matter might be referred to the Determination of the House of Commons.

The Council for the Mayor declining to advise him on this Occasion and leaving the Court, which then was in the sole possession of Sir R.W. and his Council, the Mayor was induced to proceed to poll Sir R.W.'s votes, and to declare the Election in his Favour.

If such Riots and Violences be countenanced, every Election may be carried by a Mob.

As the letter was not signed it is difficult to determine whether the election played out exactly the way it was described and it should be noted that a further letter appeared days later, again anonymous, denying that such rioting and intimidation had occurred. In a long and rambling response, printed in *Lloyd's Evening Post* in early April, the writer, who might even have been Sir Rowland himself, staunchly defended the proceedings that had taken place on polling day. The writer claimed that the three candidates had met at the mayor's house the day before the election and agreed that the following morning votes would be polled ten at a time so that ten of Lord Galway's and Henry Strachey's supporters would go first, followed by ten of Sir Rowland's and so on – these were the days before the secret ballot. The letter writer, who simply signed it 'a Constant Reader', claimed that voting took place 'without any molestation or disturbance, and without the acclamations of the populace assembled in the streets, as is usual in Elections'. He went on to claim that when the mayor counted up the votes there was no disturbance in the hall and no complaint 'on any side that any voters were hindered from coming to poll'. The correspondent added that constables guarded the doors to the hall armed with staves and halberds. He did concede that the windows of a nearby Alderman's house were smashed in and as a result the polling was indeed adjourned for a short time, but when it resumed it proceeded 'without any disturbance or noise' (excepting the one person who the writer conceded had been beaten up, though he suggested it was probably the victim's fault!).

Voting was adjourned until the next day as several supporters of Lord Galway and Mr Strachey were yet to vote. The following day, on Sir Rowland's arrival at the town hall, the writer explained that the baronet was shocked to learn that Strachey and Lord Galway had composed a letter complaining about the proceedings, alleging the tumult described above. The gist of the letter was that voters were too scared to return to cast their votes and in the end only twenty more votes were cast, some for Sir Rowland, fewer for Lord Galway and Strachey. Without any further voters, the mayor had no choice but to declare for Lord Galway and Sir Rowland.

However, the complaints of Galway, Strachey and Walsh persisted, and on 29 November, following an enquiry conducted by the House

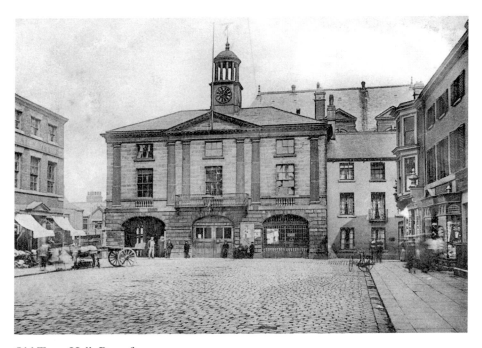

Old Town Hall, Pontefract.

of Commons, the *Leeds Intelligencer* reported that the result had been declared void and that 'a new writ is issued out for a fresh election.' The new poll took place on 5 December and the same candidates stood once more, though this time Sir Rowland's brother, Edward, also put himself on the ballot, and the Leeds paper announced the result a few days later.

> *Pontefract, Dec. 6* Yesterday came on the election for Members to serve in Parliament for this Borough: The candidates were, Sir Rowland Winn, Edward Winn, Esq, Lord Galway, and Henry Strachey, Esq; for the two first of these Gentlemen the inhabitants, householders of Pontefract voted to the number of 349; for the two latter, only such voted as were, or pretended to be, entitled to burgage-tenements within the borough. All those who voted as inhabitant-householders were rejected by the Mayor and the number of burgage-tenants appeared on the Mayor's book at the close of the poll on Tuesday evening to be as under:
>
> Sir Rowland Winn – 25
> Edward Winn – 21
> Lord Gallway – 183
> Henry Strachey – 179
>
> So that Lord Galway and Mr Strachey were returned by the Mayor.

This was a personal tragedy for Sir Rowland, who so coveted a seat in Parliament. The inhabitants of Pontefract were devastated and continued to support the baronet for several years to come. A report in the *Leeds Intelligencer* on 14 March 1769 shows in just how much affection he was held.

> We hear from Pontefract, that Tuesday last, being the birthday of Sir Rowland, it was observed there with the greatest demonstrations of joy. The morning was ushered in with ringing of bells, the evening concluded with bonfires, &c. and a grand ball, where the ladies were dressed in yellow, and decorated with ribbons of that colour; each having a large spring of Whin (Furze) in full bloom in her breast, and

another upon her head, in imitation of a pompon. A numerous body of the inhabitants also assembled at the Red Lyon, where many local healths were drank, and amongst the rest, the following, 'May the Light of Pontefract Liberty never be put out by an East-Indian Extinguisher [a reference to Henry Strachey who could be relied upon to support the faggot voters' interests in the East India Company in exchange for their votes].'

The same day one John Otley, a joiner at Pontefract, to shew his zeal for the cause of Pontefract-Liberty, had his child christened by the name of WINN. He had his house also decorated both within and without with Whins in full bloom.

Later that year, a Richard Otley of Pontefract baptized his son Monkton Walsh Otley, presumably in honour of the other major burgess holders. Brothers supporting opposing sides of the argument, perhaps? Or just their little joke?

Sir Rowland tried to become the Member for Pontefract again, firstly in 1774. On that occasion the townsfolk didn't much like his insistence at being allowed to hand-pick his supporting candidate and consequently he didn't stand. But in 1784, when he did manage to get his name on the ballot paper, he came in last place, the householders finally getting their favoured man in the person of John Smyth, who won easily.

A letter to Sir Rowland, from his son, Rowland, dated 21 June 1784, written from Nostell when the boy was just nine, described the most recent election.

Dear Papa,
Your antagonist with his colleague, I suppose have carried the day. I hear a report of Mr Smith being likely to get a seat in the house of peers which for your sake I wish. For I think there would then be no doubt of your succeeding him in his place, should you be inclined to offer yourself candidate for it.

I am dear Papa, your most affectionate and dutiful son R Winn
Nostell June 21 1784

Market Place, Pontefract, showing the Red Lion public house in the centre of the image with wagons in front of the building. The façade, dating back to 1776, was designed by Robert Adam for his employer, Sir Rowland Winn.

The death of the 5th Baronet

But it was not to be. A year later, on 20 February 1785, disaster struck when Sir Rowland, journeying to London, died at Retford, apparently the victim of a coach accident that may have been a result of poor weather. The *Leeds Intelligencer*, printed on 22 March 1785, stated:

> a metrological correspondent assures us from observation, that from the 18th of October till the 14th instant, which is a period of 143 days, there have been only 26 in which the thermometer has not been from 1 to 18 degrees and a ½ below the freezing point, which is a more constant succession of cold weather than has been known in this climate.

A notice confirming the death appeared in many provincial newspapers on 27 February, which read:

> On Sunday last died suddenly, at Retford, in Nottinghamshire, on his way to London, Sir Rowland Winn, Bart. of Nostall, in Yorkshire, in the prime of his life. He has left a disconsolate lady and two children, a son about 10 years old, a promising youth, and a daughter, a fine young lady, about 15.

Catherine Cappe said that the baronet had 'died wretchedly at an inn'. Perhaps the coach crashed through the door, or maybe Sir Rowland was outside the inn when disaster struck, or possibly he did not die in a coach accident. Whatever the circumstances, it brought an unexpected end to his baronetcy at just forty-five years old.

Already isolated and marginalized at Nostell during the long periods when her husband was away from home, the foreign 'milady', Dame Sabine Louise Winn, was now truly alone. Her mother had died in 1779, bringing an end to their regular correspondence by letter, followed by the death of her father a year later. Now in the wake of Sir Rowland's demise, letters poured in offering condolences, such as one written on 24 February 1785, just four days after the baronet's death. It was from 'Mrs Robert Milnes' of Wakefield (Esther Milnes, née Shore), whose own husband, a local merchant, had died in 1771. Mrs Milnes presented her 'respectful compliments and condolence to Lady Winn and sympathies with her distress upon the late awful event'. Another letter was from Deborah Dering, whose husband, Sir Edward Dering, MP for New Romney, was a first cousin of Sabine's late husband, the 5th Baronet. In a rather gloomy missive, she wrote that it was 'absurd' to 'attempt to give consolation … for alas! even time cannot heal a wound of this nature.' She added: 'Nothing but a firm resolution to support ourselves the best in our power under the deepest affliction can be done and this for the sake of our dear children, I am satisfied providence will support you in.' The 'great distance' that separated Lady Dering from Sabine was regretted (the Derings lived in Kent) for, she wrote, 'I fear I am deprived of being of any use any way.' She ended her letter by hoping that Sabine's children, 'Miss Winn and your son', were enjoying good health.

Sabine eventually responded to the Derings on 11 July. Her reply referred to a ring sent to Sir Edward 'as a memorial of the late deceased'. Rather curtly, the note concluded: 'Her ladyship is very well – as also her dear children, who beg he will accept their kindest respects.'

There were also exchanges of letters between Sabine and her husband's sisters. Charlotte wrote from her home in Cavendish Square, London to express her shock and sorrow at her brother's death on 2 March 1785, beginning her letter, 'My dear sister.' She continued: 'Great, very great indeed, is my affliction on this melancholy event,' going on to describe the loss of her brother as a shock 'beyond anything I ever met with'.

Hardly expecting to receive a reply, Charlotte begged Sabine to 'direct her steward to write to me as the only comfort I can receive will be to hear of the welfare of yourself and the dear children.' Two days later, Sabine's brother-in-law, Sir George Strickland, wrote a letter in which he lamented 'the loss of the acquaintance begun on your first arrival in England and have since been much concerned by being deprived from cultivating a friendship with your children.' Sir George ended his letter by offering Sabine and her children his and Lady Strickland's 'comfort or assistance', for he was sure that 'no one would be more truly attentive to it than ourselves.'

On the same day as Sir George wrote, his wife also sent Sabine a letter in which she referred to one she had written the previous Friday, when she had extended the hand of friendship. Impatient for a reply, she acknowledged that 'there is nothing more difficult than to discover even the Sun when

Cavendish Square, Wigmore Street, where Charlotte Winn lived. From *Picturesque London*, by Percy Hetherington Fitzgerald and published in 1890.

veiled by dark clouds,' but added that when the clouds dispersed the light would allow Sabine to examine Lady Strickland's heart, and when she did so she would find it was not composed of 'bad materials'. She urged Sabine to let her and Sir George visit Nostell and not to 'let false prejudices mislead you'. 'The moment we have your permission,' Lady Strickland continued, 'we shall leave no time in attending you.'

But Sabine wanted to be left alone, for she had become something of a recluse. When her own mother was dying in Switzerland she hadn't rushed to her bedside, preferring the safety of Nostell's walls and sending her husband in her stead.

According to a letter Charlotte wrote to Sabine on 21 May, Sabine had at least welcomed her offer of friendship, but it was to be carried on from a distance for an invitation to Nostell was not forthcoming. Charlotte wondered whether Sabine might journey to see her in London.

Should you ever undertake such a journey, I hope to be so situated that I have the happiness of your company under my roof without fear of giving offence, for believe me my dear friend, the seeing [of] you in any place will be a real pleasure to me. Though I flatter myself with the hopes of soon having the satisfaction of hearing either from yourself or my niece. Yet I cannot dispense without returning you my sincere thanks with my pen as an acknowledgment for all your friendly kindness to me.

Charlotte also wrote of having had a copy made of 'that picture of my dear brother and your ladyship … being a pleasing renewal to the eye, though not wanting in sensation to the mind, having too sensibly felt the loss of my dear deceased brother, whose memory I shall ever revere.' The original picture was painted in 1767 by Hugh Douglas Hamilton, an Irish portraitist. It shows the couple in Nostell's Library, Sabine resting her arm on her husband's shoulder, as he stands in a relaxed pose, leaning against the mahogany desk by Chippendale, clutching a painting and exposing his impressive collection of books to the spectator. At this time, the painting was housed at St James's Square, Sir Rowland's London home, which Sabine sold soon after her husband's death. So the painting was within easy access when Charlotte, who lived nearby, desired a copy of it. The original is now in the very library at Nostell that it depicts, and it seems it was conveyed there by Charlotte, who had one further request to make in her letter.

I sincerely wish dear Lady Winn, you could sum up resolution enough to part with your daughter for a year or two, to come to some private houses here in town who take in a few young ladies about her age. It would be a great advantage and improvement to her. I have known several young ladies who have been at those houses and found great benefit by it and if you rely on my judgment and attachment to her you may depend upon it. I would pay her all the attention it was possible, and acquaint you in what manner she proceeds … and might have an opportunity of having any masters for introduction that your Ladyship thought proper.

Interestingly, at the end of the letter Charlotte wrote that she'd heard that James Paine (the architect, or possibly his son and namesake) had been at Nostell when he had brought news 'that Sir George and Lady Strickland are going to make some stay there.' They were certainly holding out for an invitation, as their earlier letter showed. However, Charlotte wrote that given Sabine's 'abhorrence of their former conduct of proceeding in my dear brother's lifetime', she doubted Sabine would host such a visit, nor gain any 'enjoyment in their company'. It seems this was a family who engaged in much in-fighting.

Replying to Charlotte's letter, Sabine wrote that whilst a meeting between the two of them would be 'no less addition to my happiness than to yours', such a pleasure, she feared, 'must for the present remain an idea,' for she could not 'summon up the resolution, neither think of leaving Nostell.'

And then she rejected the idea of sending Esther, by now in her seventeenth year, to London. Whilst acknowledging the 'many advantages my daughter might reap from spending a little time in London', which would 'enlarge her ideas of the world', she was 'unwilling'. Unwilling, that is, 'to have her beyond the reach of my own eye and inspection,' adding, cryptically, 'for reasons I cannot mention by letter.'

Christopher Todd wrote that Esther was a difficult child who Sabine found hard to control. He cited a letter from Shepley Watson, the Winns' solicitor, who wrote that it was feared Esther was ready to elope from Nostell with a glazier's apprentice, and that 'post horses [have] paraded before the gates at Nostell night after night to convey her away.' Whilst Watson was writing a few years after Sabine's exchange with Charlotte, it seems that her mother was happier to think of her locked away at Nostell as would-be Prince Charmings dithered beyond the gates.

As for the threatened visit to Nostell by Sir George and Lady Strickland, Sabine claimed to know nothing of this, and wrote that she did not 'know that James Paine was even at Nostell.' Such a visit by her in-laws 'can never take place,' she asserted. 'I spurn at every idea of the kind,' she continued, 'and when I call to mind their former manner of proceedings I cannot but abhor their conduct too much to ever have the least enjoyment in their society.' In a postscript, Sabine told Charlotte that 'Miss Winn of Bath', i.e. Mary Winn, Charlotte's sister, had written to say she was in Yorkshire and would like to wait on her. Sabine said that her response had been simple and to the point: 'At present I do not see company.'

Two years later, on 16 August 1787, Sir Rowland's will was partially proved. He'd written the will in June 1779 and appointed as his executrix Lady Winn, who he said was 'esteemed and much beloved'. Major focus fell on the testator's plans for the education of his son, who was in his twelfth year by the time probate had begun.

My earnest desire is that the education of my son and heir may be particularly attended to and that it may be very liberal and such as is not only proper to make him a gentleman but also a man of business which will be happiness to himself and useful to his neighbours. And to attain these ends I desire that when he shall have attained the age of seven years that he may be committed to the care of a private tutor whose only employment shall be the education of my son. And for his care therein I desire he may be paid half-yearly the sum of one hundred and fifty pounds besides meat, lodgings and all necessaries at my house at Nostel.

And I recommend the Reverend William Sheepshanks of Leeds as a very proper person for such charge. But if he refuses to accept thereof then such other person as my said trustees shall approve for learning and morality with power for them to appoint any other person … until he attain his age of fifteen years. And that he then go to some publick school attended by his private tutor who I desire may overlook his actions when he is not in the immediate care of his master.

He furthered desired that his son attend school for a year, then go to university in Cambridge for two years, followed by travels through 'England, Scotland and Wales' accompanied by his tutor. After this, Sir Rowland felt his son would benefit from visiting Lausanne, Switzerland, just as he had done, then to 'such other places and countries' as Sir Rowland's trustees advised. For the continued tutelage of his son, Sir Rowland made available £300, plus expenses to be paid until his son and heir reached the age of twenty-one. As it turned out the appointed tutor died shortly into the late baronet's plan, and Sabine attempted to keep her son at Nostell, where she would continue his education, contrary to the express wishes her husband had written in his will. The case ended up in Chancery, with threats of prison made against Sabine, whose health was failing and who had to wade through mounting bills 'bequeathed' to her by her husband, who had rarely paid his creditors on time. Sabine, who was fast becoming a total recluse, withdrew from society, with little to amuse her to pass the time, though she did enjoy compiling 'receipts', that is to say, collections of recipes and medicinal cures that she found in newspapers and through word of mouth. She copied these into several bound volumes, which survive in the Nostell archive. To provide some respite from the interfamilial strife, the next chapter comprises a selection of these receipts, some of which you can even try at home, though if eighteenth-century cuisine and remedies result in any serious illnesses, injuries or even deaths, then blame Sabine Winn and not the present writer!

Chapter 3

Sabine Winn's Receipts

Ginger-Bread

Ingredients:
Three pounds of fine flour
A pint of honey
A pound of sugar
A little sack [fortified wine]
Ginger
Coriander
Caraway seeds
Candied lemon and citron peel
Butter for greasing your pans

Method:
To three pound of fine flour take a pint of honey, one pound of white sugar, make 'em boyle and scum it clean. Let it stand a little and put in a little sack to the honey and sugar then stir it into the flour. Put in your ginger, coriander and what caraway seeds you please, beaten and sifted and add some slices of candied lemon and citron peel and caraway comfits. And when 'tis mingled set it against the fire to rise 'till your oven is hot. Butter your pans very little and if they are not a little buttered they will not come out. Set 'em in a quick oven – about an hour will bake 'em.

A gingerbread seller, from *Memoirs of Bartholomew Fair*.

Lady Winn's Mother's Fritters

Ingredients:
Eight eggs
Pint of thin (single) cream
A pinch of salt
Cinnamon to taste
Plain flour
Four tablespoons of fortified wine
Some pippins
A good store of hogs fat [lard]

Method:
Take eight eggs and discard four whites. Beat 'em very well then take a pint of thin cream warmed and put with your eggs. Stir 'em well together with a little salt and cinnamon. Then put in the flour till your batter is thick enough. Beat it well and let it stand covered near your fire to rise. Then beat it well again and put in four spoonsful of sack [fortified wine]. Then slice some pippins very thin and put 'em in the batter and take 'em out with a spoon, every slice by itself. Fry 'em with good store of Hogs-fat, very hot.

Plumb Cake

Ingredients:
3½ pounds of the finest flour
The yolks of 12 eggs
A quart of cream
A pound of butter
½ a pound of loaf-sugar
½ an ounce of large mace
½ pint of the best ale
A little damask rose water
3½ pounds of currants

Method:
Take 3 pound & a half of the finest flour, well dry'd, the yolkes of 12 well-beaten eggs, & a quart of boyl'd cream. Put a pound of Butter to it, half a pound of loafe-sugar, mixed with yo'r flour, half an ounce of large mace, half a pint of the best ale, & a little damask rose water. Make a round hole in the flour & put all these ingredients into it. Then strew some of the same flour into the hole, the thickness of half an inch. Then let it stand 'till it workes over, then mix it up & take 3 pound & a half of currance & put into it as you mix it. Clap it on a paper, well-butter'd with a hoop about it. Set it into the oven & let it stand an hour & 3 quarters.

Christmas Pyes

Ingredients:
Tongue
Beef suet, equal to the weight of the tongue
Nutmeg, clover, mace and sugar to taste
¼ of a pound of raisins
Candied orange and lemon peel
One citron
Raw lemon peel
Juice of two lemons
Six tablespoons of Canary wine [fortified wine from Spain or the Canary Islands]
Handful of currants

Method:
Boyle a tongue 'till it will peel. When 'tis cold cut it in pieces (leave out the roots) and chop it very small with the weight of very good beef suet. Then put in a little salt and add what nutmeg, clover, mace and sugar you please. Then stone a quarter of a pound of raisins and cut them very small and stir 'em well into the meat. Then cut some candied orange and lemon peel pretty small with some citron and put in with it a little raw lemon peel shred very small. Squeeze in the juice of two lemons. Put in six spoonsful

of Canary [wine] or more, and as many currants as you please. Be sure you stir all well together so that it may have a true mixture. Put the sack [wine] in just before you fill 'em. Bake 'em in a pretty quick oven. When they are almost done the fat will swim on top. When it begins to sink they are ready. If you make your pyes with mutton then boyle a leg (half is enough) and cut it from the sinews and skins, and to every pound of mutton put a pound and a quarter of beef-suet, chopped small and season it to your taste.

Champagne Gooseberries

Ingredients:
A pound of gooseberries (unstoned)
A pound of sugar
Half a pint of water

Method:
To a pound of gooseberries, before they are stoned, take a pound of sugar and half a pint of water. Boil the sugar and water very well and scum it. Then having your gooseberries stoned and split as little as you can, put them in and cover them. Boil them 'til they cook clear, then put them in to glasses, then strain your liquor upon them. Four ounce pots are better than glasses.

The Duchess of Norfolk's Punch

Ingredients:
Eight lemons
Eight oranges
A gallon of brandy
Two gallons of fair water
Four pounds of fine sugar
Whites of eight eggs

Method:
Take the paring of eight lemons and as many oranges, pared very thin. Steep 'em in a gallon of brandy and keep closed for 24 hours. Then take two gallons of fair water (or something more if you like it smaller). Add

An obese gouty man drinking punch. By J. Gillray in 1799 and published by H. Humphrey in *Catalogue of Political and Personal Satires.*

four pound of fine sugar and clarify it while it boyles with the whites of eight eggs. Let it boil a quarter of an hour and skim it very well. Let it stand 'til 'tis cold then strain the brandy from the parings and mix it with the clarified water and put in the juice of the lemons and oranges, which were pared. Then put it in a barrel, stop it close for three months and then bottle it. If it does not come fine in that time, keep it longer in the barrel.

To make Orange Wine

Ingredients:
Three gallons of water
Six pounds of sugar
The whites of two eggs
100 Seville oranges
Yeast

Method:

Take three gallons of water and six pounds of sugar. Boyle 'em half an hour, then scum it. Then clarifye it with the white of two eggs and when 'tis cool put in the juice and outward rinds of a quart of a hundred Seville oranges. Work it with yeast and let it work for twenty-eight hours in an open tub. Then strain it and put it into a vessel and in a fortnight's time draw it off.

A Syrup to Kill a Kanker in ye Mouth

Ingredients:

Herbs (a handful of each):

    Grace

    Red Sage

    Honey Suckle Leaves

    Rosemary Tops

Burnt Alum, finely beaten

Honey

Any syrup, as preferred

Isaac Swainson promoting his 'Velnos syrup'. Ironically, perhaps, considering Thomas Gargrave's preferred 'poison', this image shows Swainson's rivals who preferred to use mercury. By Thomas Rowlandson in 1789 and published by W. Fores.

Method:
Stamp the herbs all together and then strain out all the juice and take a
good quantity of burnt alum. Take also a quantity of honey and put 'em
into your juice making it pretty thick. Stir it well and put into a pot and
keep it closed. And when you use it rub the gums and sore places with it.
You may wash your mouth first with water and then rub it with syrup (any
of 'em will do it). The water will heal sore breasts that have a canker if you
warm it and wash the breast with it when 'tis sore.

A Dyet Drink to Cure all Manner of Hurts and Wounds

Ingredients:
Two ounces of sarsaparilla
Two ounces of sassafras wood
One ounce of china roots
One ounce of tormentil roots
Half a pound of liquorish
A quarter of a pound of aniseeds
Two ounces of china
Half-an-ounce of rhubarb

Two good handfuls of:
    Ladies mantle
    Marshmallow roots
    Sanicle
    Betony
    Columbine roots
    Egremony
    Scabious
    Mouse ear
    Colt's foot
    Herb Robert

A quart of white wine
Two ounces of senna
Half an ounce of sliced rhubarb

Method:
Take all the woods and herbs, shred the roots and the herbs. Put 'em into three gallons of running water, boyle 'em 'till half be consumed then strain 'em thro' a colander. Take the ingredients and put to 'em again two gallons of running water. Boyle the better half away, strain it hard thro' a coarse cloth & put the first and second liquor with the white wine and let it set. Scum it and when 'tis off the fire put it to the senna and rhubarb. Stir 'em together and cover it. Drink blood warm in quantities of half-a-pint thereof in a morning, at five in the afternoon and on going to bed.

An Aprrov'd Medicine to Drive the Scurvy or any other Ill Humour out of a Man's Body

Ingredients:
A quart of running water
The flesh of three lemons
Two or three sprigs of rosemary
A quantity of sliced figs
Some raisins of the sun (stoned)
A few aniseeds (bruised)
Some sliced liquorish
Powdered white sugar candy

Method:
Boyle all these together to a pint, then put in as much white sugar candy (powered) as will make it a syrup. Then let 'em boyle together and scum it. Let the party drink of it two spoonsful at a time, twice or thrice in a day.

Dr Lower's Receipt for a Cold

Ingredients:
Two spoonsful of the best salad oil
A quarter of a pound of brown sugar candy, finely beaten with the juice of half a lemon

Wrapped up and suffering from
a cold. Published in 1833 by
G. Tregear.

Method:
Mix these together and take of it at your pleasure.

To Heal any Cut

Ingredients:
Sixpenny worth of oil of spike
The same of train oil, otherwise whale oil

Method:
Put them together in a glass. Drop it into the sore and bind it up.

To Cure Convulsion Fits in those that have had Nine in a Day

Ingredients:
Equal quantities of:
    Raw onions
    Black pepper

Mithridate, or syrup of oil of amber
Black cherry water
Peony, clove and gillyflower syrup
Peony root necklace

Method:
Take the ingredients stamped pretty small and lay it at the soles of the feet. Force 'em not to take anything inwardly, but anoint the wrists, the palms of the hands, the temples and the nostrils with Mithridate, amber being too hot for a child. Between the fits let 'em drink black cherry water, sweetened with peony, clove and gillyflower syrup. For a week's time after the fit give two or three spoonsful of black cherry water for it. Last of all let 'em wear a single peony root necklace. Note: Always avoid giving syrup of violets, but syrup of roses and succory together are ever good. This may be given to children of any age or to men or women. Syrup of oil of amber may be given instead of Mithridate.

To Cause an Easy Labour

Ingredients:
Six ounces of brown sugar candy, beaten into powder
A quarter of a pound of raisins of the sun (stoned)
Two ounces of dates (unstoned and sliced)
An ounce of aniseeds (bruised)
A quarter of an ounce of cowslip flowers
A dram of rosemary flowers
Two quarts of white wine

Method:
Take ten or twelve days before her looking [ready to give birth] the listed ingredients. Put these into a fine lawn bag with a flint stone (that it may sink) into the white wine. Let it steep 24 hours and after take of it in the morning, at four in the afternoon and in the evening. The quantity is a wine glass full.

To Cure Madnesse in Dogs, Cattle &c.

Ingredients:
A handful of rosemary
A handful of marigolds
A pint of milk
An ounce of madder root
Enough wheat meal to make a paste

Method:
Shred the flowers small and boyle 'em in the milk 'till half is consumed with the madder. Then make it into paste with wheat meal. Give it to the dog in a morning fasting him for two days before the full change of the moon.

For the eyes

Ingredients:
A like quantity of
Ground ivy
Celandines
Daisies
A little sugar candy
A little rose water
A feather

Method:
Take ground ivy, celandines & daisies of each a like quantity stampt & strain'd, a little sugar candy & rose water & put 'em together & drop it with a feather into your eye. It takes away all manner of inflammations, spots, webs, smarting or any other griefe whatsoever incident to your eyes. 'Tis approved to be the best medicine in the world.

Chapter 4

Esther, the 6th Baronet, and the Williamsons

[She] writes [in a] beautiful hand, spells so accurately, arranges her ideas with such precision, and is mistress of French and Italian, and who has a competent knowledge of music, dancing &c. [She] can never be called deficient in education, since she is infinitely better educated than free fourths of the present young ladies.

This is a description of Lady Esther Sabina Winn, daughter of the late 5th Baronet and his Swiss wife, Lady Sabine Winn, who evidently had a bright future of wealth and privilege to look forward to. But she chose a different path.

On 9 January 1793, against her mother's wishes, and probably having eloped, Lady Esther married John Williamson in the Lancashire mill town of Manchester. Several documents in Nostell's archive suggest that the groom was merely a lowly baker. What a terribly inappropriate husband for a baronet's daughter. That said, he was described in the marriage entry as a gentleman. The marriage took place at what is now Manchester Cathedral following the granting of a marriage licence. The bond and marriage licence allegation also describe him as a gentleman. Their first child, a son, John Williamson, was born on 27 March 1794, and he was baptized in Manchester on 15 May that year, the entry once again stating that his father was a gentleman. Another son, Charles, followed, and he was baptized on 12 July 1795. A daughter, named Elfrida, was baptized on 10 July 1798, but she died a month later and was buried on 10 August, though another daughter would be born later. The following month, Lady Sabine Winn, whose health had deteriorated, died of rheumatic gout. It was said that she had 'become very stout and was wheeled about in a quaint big wheeled chair, which was preserved in old Nostell days,' and had to use poles to exercise.

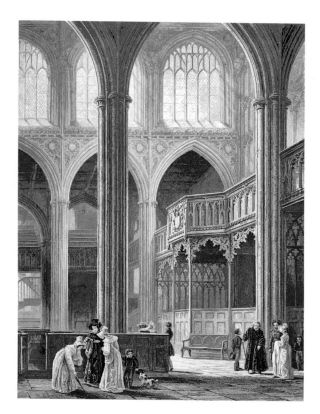

Manchester Cathedral,
formerly the Collegiate
Church of St Mary,
St Denys and St George, as
shown in a sketch published
in 1834 in volume two of
*History of the Foundations in
Manchester's Christ's College,
Cheetham's Hospital, and the
Free Grammar School*, by
Samuel Hibbert and others.

In the years before her death Lady Winn had made clear her feelings towards her daughter, and her daughter's choice of husband, who, we learn from an endorsement on a letter written by Esther to the Nostell family solicitor, Shepley Watson, wasn't any old baker, but 'the baker at Nostell'.

Was this true? In 1887, T.G. Wright, the Winns' long serving family doctor, compiled for his children and grandchildren an unpublished manuscript titled *Reminiscences of Nostell*, in which he documented his many years' service at the house. He recalled stories he'd been told 'by one who knew the details', including tales about Esther (who was also known as Sabina) from before her marriage. In these tales he confirmed the supposed occupation of Mr Williamson:

the young lady [was] nurtured amid unhappy surroundings, isolated in her social position, and probably left in injudicious guardianships. What

The Obelisk Lodge at Nostell Priory, formerly the entrance to the grounds.

wonder that she was wayward and headstrong! She first formed an undesirable attachment to a young man from Doncaster, who was employed in plumber's work on the premises, described to me (by one who knew the details) as a very handsome young fellow, with whom Miss Sabina corresponded; but their letters were discovered and intercepted, and the flirtation was put an end to.

I know nothing further of Miss Esther Sabina Winn's story, only that it is said she left Nostell in 1792 or 3, (when about two & twenty), with a Mr Williamson a domestic stated to be a baker, also a handsome young man, for Manchester, where they were married; and in 1794 a son John was born; another son Charles in 1795, and in June 1799, a daughter, Louisa.

Letters from Aunt Mary

Baker, or indeed, butcher, candlestick maker, or provincial gentleman, John and Esther would live in perfectly mundane circumstances in chilly Manchester, where John would suffer continual poor health and Esther would have few friends. Esther's spinster aunt, Mary Winn, had written a letter to her niece in May 1797, when Esther's mother was still alive, in which she wrote that Lady Winn had tried to turn Esther against her relations, describing this as a cruel action. Mary's letter is interesting in that it becomes clear from the start that Esther had never met her Aunt Mary:

> I make no doubt that you will be greatly surprised to receive a letter from one who is entirely a stranger to you, I mean personally so, though not by name, and very sorry I am to think, so near a relation as your father's own sister, has never been allowed to have any kind of connection with those who are so nearly allied as you and your brother.

Mary was not one to refrain from speaking her mind and made sure that Esther (or Sabina, as she called her) knew that she was well aware of Esther's 'mother's conduct in every respect'. She was 'particularly' conscious of Lady Winn's endeavours 'to prejudice you against all your relations, which was a cruel action, and can say with the greatest truth we wished to have befriended you, had it been in our power.' Mary explained that letters she'd written to Esther had evidently been kept from her whilst 'the bad opinion of us all which was imprinted in your mind gave you a dislike, which was a very natural surmise.' She went on:

> I have frequently made many enquiries about you, since you settled in Manchester, and it has given me the utmost pleasure to be informed how well you have conducted yourself and are respected by all your acquaintances, which I hope will always be your study to obtain, for in every situation in life, it is necessary to gain the good opinion of everyone, and I hope you will never 'ere from it. And that you are happy and comfortable is my sincere wish. I never could know 'till very lately your right address, although I frequently heard of you, but a melancholy event having taken place in our family, it made it necessary to find out in what part of Manchester you did reside.

This melancholy event was the death, a month earlier, of Mary's sister Charlotte, who had been bedridden for the last months of her life owing to a long-standing illness. Mary was writing to tell Esther that Charlotte had left her a mother-of-pearl pocket case, inlaid with gold. Charlotte's will also reveals that her bequest to Esther included the copy of the Hugh Douglas Hamilton painting of her parents, which Charlotte had commissioned. Mary promised to send these bequests to Esther as soon as Esther wrote back to confirm that she would like to continue to correspond with her aunt and 'what family you have', ending her letter: 'Dear Sabina, your very sincere friend and affectionate Aunt Mary Winn.'

Their correspondence did indeed continue, Mary's letters to Esther surviving in the Nostell archive. Esther had obviously replied to Mary's initial approach within days, for another letter from Mary, dated 23 May 1797, thanked Esther for sending news of her family, Mary telling her:

> it gave all your friends the utmost pleasure to hear you and your family were all well, which is one of the greatest blessings on Earth, adding to it happiness and a comfortable competence, both of which I hope you enjoy.

Mary also told Esther that if she ever found herself passing through Manchester again, 'I will most certainly endeavour to see you.' She added, 'believe me you have never been forgotten by any of those who were not allowed to approach the House at Nostell.'

In another letter Mary asked Esther whether she ever heard from family at Nostell, hoping 'they are kind to you', but added that she never received word from there, 'nor should not know there were any such people living, was I not obliged to write sometimes to Mr Watson [the family solicitor] for the money your brother pays me.' Mary wondered whether Longsight, where Esther and her family lived, was a single house, or a village, obviously having never heard of the suburb of Manchester that Esther called home.

In subsequent letters, Mary constantly apologized for being a poor correspondent, though she had just lost another relative, so this was perhaps forgivable. Her own aunt, her father's sister (also called Mary), had died in her eighty-sixth year, having made Mary her executrix, and it was this duty that had prevented her from writing regularly to Esther, though when she did she repeated her promises to visit Manchester one day.

The exchange of letters continued and Esther confirmed to her aunt that she had not heard from anybody at Nostell since the day she'd left.

On learning of this, Mary hoped that 'the malice of that part of the family does not extend so far as to deprive you of what is your own, but pays you regularly as they would at the time of your marriage.'

Mary tended to come across as a little nosey when she turned to these enquiries, having promised in an earlier letter to drop the subject, and never mention it again, only to return to it in most of her letters, though Esther obviously encouraged Mary to do so via her replies. Thank goodness for that, because the contents of Mary's letters were always fiery and she was never afraid to stoke that fire:

> it is no curiosity that makes me enquire about it, but knowing too well your mother's hatred to you and all the family. I am sorry to say she is equal to anything that she thought would distress those to whom she took a dislike. And your brother, she has so great an influence over him, which I am sorry for, as some people say he has a good heart, which if true, she will I am sure, poison him.

Sir Rowland, the 6th Baronet, was a man by now, but in the years following his father's death the matter of his education had become a case heard in the Court of Chancery. This was because his mother was found not to be following the wishes made explicit in her late husband's will, specifically in relation to the former baronet's wish that old Reverend Sheepshanks be handed the post of the boy's tutor. In 1790, five years after the 5th Baronet's death, and when his successor was only fifteen, Charles Mellish of Badsworth Hall, a former MP for Pontefract, wrote, at the request of Sabine herself, to John Maddocks of Lincoln's Inn, offering his opinion on the case, and in doing so provided a summary of the education young Sir Rowland had so far received, which was described as defective. Referring to the case, Mellish stated that a Reverend Leech had attended Sir Rowland for about three years and had then, rather unhelpfully, dropped down dead. Mellish was not sure how proficient the boy had become under Reverend Leech and explained that it was expected Reverend Sheepshanks would be the natural successor, given he'd been nominated in the will. It seems Leech was not a successful tutor, or as Mellish speculated, perhaps 'Sir Rowland would not learn.' Either way, Mellish was at pains to point out that 'Lady Winn was certainly not the person to blame.'

Sheepshanks, it seemed, had swanned off abroad and upon his return chose a different line of work (perhaps he did not care to become mixed up with the Winns!). As outlined in the will, young Sir Rowland was supposed to go with his tutor, whoever that was, to spend one year at a public school, but unfortunately, whilst he had a good heart, he was evidently a bit thick, or 'very backward in his learning', so much so that Mellish thought it would be 'an absurdity to place him there'. In summary, Mellish said:

> if he were placed in the lower school at Eton, it is impossible that he could have submitted to it, and, if placed too high, he would only have been what the universities call, crammed with learning, without any foundation, and would have blundered on to college or abroad.

So what was to be done? Mellish asked Maddocks.

> Lady Winn and Sir Rowland are both sensible that 'tis necessary he should attend to his education and Sir Rowland is very desirous of improving himself in the mode he himself chalks out, which is to attend daily the Reverend Mr Simpson of Hemsworth, a clergyman of great sense and learning, who is very much respected in this part, for so many hours as Mr Simpson shall think necessary either at Nostell or at Hemsworth.

In other words, Sir Rowland was to stay by his mother's side, for Hemsworth is hardly far from Nostell, the modern entrance to the house being at the crossroads with Garmill Road, which leads directly to Hemsworth. Mellish didn't seem overly confident but agreed it was a plan 'worth trying' because Sir Rowland seemed fond of Reverend Simpson, and anyway, it was the only 'feasible plan'. If this failed Mellish thought there would be nothing else to attempt, for the lad was headstrong and, as he put it, composed of a 'very quick understanding, who may be induced to apply, but whom compulsion would only make obstinate.' He concluded his letter to Maddocks by suggesting that they try this plan for at least a year, or a year and a half, and if there were signs of improvement then they could send Sir Rowland to college and abroad 'with a proper tutor, which he seems desirous of doing, when he thinks himself qualified for that purpose.'

A few years later, Esther's husband, John Williamson, wrote to her from Beverley, where he was staying during his travels. Whilst at York, he'd heard about an incident at Nostell that had occurred on Sir Rowland's birthday. Evidently there was a 'little to-do' between the baronet and a young lady whose mother had been desirous of presenting her as a possible mate. An opportunity had arisen 'for the young gentleman to get acquainted with her,' but Sabine had got to know about it and had 'ordered the daughter away immediately.' Clearly Lady Winn wanted her son all to herself and was quite prepared to see off any oncomers before Sir Rowland had the chance to say hello.

In July 1798, just weeks before Lady Winn passed away, Esther received another letter from her aunt Mary in which she asked Esther whether she'd received all the money she was owed from Nostell. For not only was she incommunicado, Esther was also being deprived of what she was owed by birthright. Mary could certainly sympathize with her having experienced the same ill-fortune herself at the hands of Esther's father. When Mary suggested that if the money hadn't been paid, 'Mr Williamson should get some sensible clever attorney to write to them and expostulate with them,' it was as if she was replaying events from earlier years, and savouring the possibility of getting one over on the estate.

Mary Winn's next letter was written a month later and by now Lady Winn was close to the end of her life. Although, as Mary pointed out, 'no relation can get to [Lady Winn's or Sir Rowland's] ear,' she had heard that Esther's mother had 'lost the use of her limbs, as to be obliged to be lifted by two people in and out of bed, I suppose from the gout.' It was at this time that Esther had buried her daughter Elfrida, and Mary, who had now visited Esther and her family, wrote that she did not think the unfortunate child 'appeared very strong when I saw her, for I observed at that time she was eighteen weeks old and had not the strength to hold up her head, which I have seen children do before that age.' In the same letter she wrote that she had heard of Lady Winn's death, not from Sir Rowland, or his steward, as was the proper way to announce such an event, but from reading about it in the newspaper, where a bland notice told her that 'Lady Winn, relict of the late Sir Rowland Winn, bart.' had died in her sixtieth year. Consequently, unaware of her passing, none of the distant relations 'put on mourning'.

Mary felt that even if Sir Rowland did not know of the custom of writing to relatives to inform them of deaths in the family, Shepley Watson, the family solicitor, should have told him to do so, it being 'cruel' that nobody had bothered to inform Esther. Mary warned Esther and her husband to be wary of Mr Watson, who she felt had attempted a conspiracy to cheat Esther out of £10,000 that was due to her from her parents' marriage settlement. Mary urged Esther to write to her brother, Sir Rowland, as soon as possible to declare her affection for him, presumably to get into his good books now the old lady was dead. 'By doing so,' Mary said, especially while his heart was softened by distress, 'you may make some impression on him and it may turn to your advantage. And if it should not you will not then have anything to blame yourself for, nor can the world do it.'

Mary couldn't resist imparting a bit of gossip that had come her way concerning Lady Winn's deathbed refusal to allow her son to send for Esther: 'I have been informed by a letter I received today out of the West Riding [that] your brother mentioned you to Lady Winn and offered to send for you, but she had forbid it.'

Perhaps this explains why Esther, upset by this remark, failed to immediately reply to her aunt, for in Mary's next letter, sent a couple of months later, she began it by saying:

> I have for some time expected to hear from you, not having had that pleasure, since the letter I wrote to you from Scarborough, wherein I recommended you to write immediately to your brother, the result of which I am really impatient to know.

Was there a will?

Mary often worried that her letters were being intercepted, and she thought perhaps this had happened to her previous missive, having not received a reply, rather than Esther simply being struck by grief. Or maybe Esther's husband was unwell, for Esther often wrote to Mary to tell her about his poor health. Whatever the reason for Esther's silence, Mary was desperate to hear whether her niece had written to Sir Rowland, begging she tell her 'to put me out of my suspense, for I must acknowledge, I do very much feel interested about you, having the welfare of yourself and family very much at heart.' Mary then speculated about whether Esther's mother had made a will. Local opinion, Mary explained, held that if Sabine had not written a will, then, because her possessions were made up of personal items rather than real estate, Esther would 'come in for a part of it'. Mary told Esther that it might be necessary to know when Esther's maternal grandmother had died so they could send for a copy of her will to see what she had said about the 'disposal of the effects she left to your mother'. She also wished that Esther was in possession of some diamonds that were once Esther's maternal grandmother's but had been left to Esther in the care of her mother, Sabine.

Mary also said she'd like to visit Esther, but because the Lancashire roads were 'so roughly bad, I had not the courage to pass over them again.' But it was the comment about Esther's grandmother's will that would turn out to be prophetic.

A few weeks later, Mary learned from Esther about the possible existence of a will written by her mother, Sabine, and she wrote about this in her next letter to Esther, penned in February 1799. From this, we learn that an unnamed source had told Esther that her mother had received £60,000 from her own mother's will, but that at Sabine's death there was only £6,000 left. The same source also informed Esther that she was to receive precisely nothing from either her mother's or grandmother's estates. Mary was reluctant to accept that Esther could be so easily disinherited, and wondered whether 'the person who informed you' (about the wills) was 'to be depended on'.

Mary was still keen to know whether Esther had written to her brother, like she had suggested. And she also asked Esther where she and John were planning to live, 'as you told me, when I had the pleasure of seeing you at Manchester, the landlord had given Mr Williamson notice to quit.'

At this time the Williamson family occupied a house at 4 Dickinson Street, where they'd lived since the births of their children. By June 1799, they would leave Manchester and relocate to Lincolnshire, but Esther received a couple more letters from her aunt before the move. The first, sent on 27 February, dealt further with the subject of Sabine Winn's will, and there was clearly still some hope that Esther's source had been mistaken and that such a will might not exist after all. If it turned out there was no will, Mary told Esther that she would be due half of her mother's estate. Mary urged Esther to apply

The bottom of Market Street, Manchester in about 1820, close to Dickinson Street, where Esther Williamson was living when she corresponded with her aunt. From *Views of Old Manchester*, published in 1885.

to the Prerogative Court at Doctors' Commons in London to request a copy of Sabine's supposed will, so she could see for herself if the rumours of her disinheritance were true. During this discourse, Mary described the Nostell solicitor, Shepley Watson, as a 'snake in the grass'. She suggested his behavior towards Esther, who had been in correspondence with Mr Watson regarding her mother's estate, 'had imprinted on my mind a bad opinion of him.' Mary specifically laid the blame for the wider family not hearing of Sabine's death at Mr Watson's door, 'for he ought to have written to everyone.' She also concluded that Sir Rowland was now under the solicitor's influence, and suggested that the new baronet was a rather weak, isolated figure, who she feared would not make a very good High Sheriff of Yorkshire (a role he was widely expected to be handed) owing to his lack of experience of any office. Presumably Mary's impressions of her nephew were entirely based on gossip and hearsay, but she went on to say, 'I frequently think he must feel himself very uncomfortable not having one person he can call his friend.' And she wanted to know what his plans for the future were and told Esther to let her know, if she heard anything juicy, adding, 'for what you say to me will never turn to your disadvantage, so you need not be afraid.'

Mary's coverage of a wide range of subject matters, all concerning Esther's private life, continued, moving on to Esther and John's domestic situation. Having obviously received a letter from Esther confirming that they were indeed giving up the Longsight house and moving to Lincolnshire, Mary wrote:

As Mr Williamson [who had been in worsening health] was concerned with the necessity of moving from Longsight, I am glad he has met with a situation that he likes. I hope the Lincolnshire air will agree better with him than the cold blast from off your terrible hills, which I have a very great overview to. If the place you have taken is very near Gainsboro' I should think it must be a flat country. I was at that place, but it is so many years ago, I have almost forgotten it. I suppose it is a farm. Is it in a town or entirely the country? How near Gainsboro' is it? And what is the name of the place?

At the end of her letter Mary casually remarked that there'd been an earthquake during the previous month, 'about 4 o'clock in the morning, which alarmed me very much,' and she was thankful it didn't cause any damage, though she wrote that it was felt in 'many parts of France, Normandy and Jersey'. Newspaper reports from the time record that such an earthquake did occur on 25 January 1799. Weather phenomena clearly on her mind, Mary also described the events of 'last Friday', when she'd been visited by one of the 'most horrendous storms of thunder, lightning, rain and hail, which lasted about an hour, and in Torbay which is in sight of this place, three men were killed and fifteen wounded by the lightning.'

Mary's last letter to Longsight was an epic, packed with family news, the author promising in her introduction to 'not leave any stone unturned'. It was written on 3 March 1799 and in it Mary explained that she'd taken it upon herself to make enquiries to discover once and for all whether or not any will had been made by Sabine Winn. And if there was a will, she wanted to know whether or not it had been proved. The response she'd received was that probate had not taken place in any of the ecclesiastical courts. The respondent had told Mary that half a year after a death was quite long enough to expect any extant will to have been proved and that Esther should write 'to her brother and request to know whether her mother had left any will and if so, to have a copy of it. And if not, to know what dividable property was in his hands.' Esther was also advised to infer that, if no will had been left, she was intending to take out administration of her mother's estate, just in case Sir Rowland felt like ignoring her enquiries. It was also suggested that she ought to have her letters drafted by 'the very best lawyer'. Mary cautioned her niece not to mention 'a syllable of the diamonds in your first letter', but to instead wait for her brother's answer first. Clearly Esther was keen to get her hands on these precious stones. But it seems so was her aunt, who added:

whenever you get the diamonds, should you wish to dispose of them, do let me know, as there is nothing where people are so likely to be impaired in, as diamonds. And I know a jeweller in London with whom I have had great dealings, and who is employed by people of first fashion and fortune and particularly by all the Yorkshire families who will give you the right price for them. And if you wish it, I will do my endeavours to sell them for you to them, for the people in the country don't know their value and by that means you may lose greatly by them. I mention this as perhaps you might be at a loss to know what to do with them. And besides the price of diamonds rises and falls as much as gold and silver does.

After a bit of gossip about Sir Rowland, Mary returned to the subject of Esther's mother's estate. 'The sooner now you enter on this business,' she said, 'I should think would be better.' Mary could not see why there should be any further delay and told Esther that she expected 'to be informed how you go on'. Mary also wanted Esther to inform Sir George Strickland, Esther's uncle, of Sir Rowland's response on the basis that Sir George had provided regular advice on the matter, and because, in truth, Mary was desperate to know the outcome and was planning a holiday, and so didn't want to risk missing an interesting letter.

Mary's next note to Esther, sent to her new home in the Lincolnshire village of Morton, was written on 23 June. By then Sir Rowland had acted. There had been a will all along, and on 29 March that year he'd had it proved at the Prerogative Court Canterbury at Doctors' Common, London.

Unbelievably, nobody bothered to tell Esther of this significant development, and she certainly hadn't heard the news by June, for the letter her aunt wrote that month made no specific mention of the matter, though she did share news of Sir Rowland's first appearance at York Assizes in his capacity as High Sheriff of Yorkshire, an office he'd attained that year. In this, he'd apparently exceeded his aunt's low expectations.

> I am sure you will be glad to hear he has behaved very properly at the assizes, and gained great credit. I hope he will now mix more in the world. All the gentleman would be very glad to take him by the hand. I heard he was much struck with a lady at York and some say he made her an offer, but was too late, she being engaged to another gentleman, and is since married to him. Her name was Barlow [possibly Eliza Barlow, who married Robert Clavering Savage at York in April that year].

Mary hoped that Esther was settled in her new home and wondered whether Mr Williamson might consider taking on a bit more land as 'growing would be a pretty amusement for him.' As for her own situation, Mary had been unsettled at her rented property in Exmouth, hoping to relocate to

Yorkshire, but without having found a suitable home, which would have to be furnished. It's clear from this small talk that neither party had learned of the major developments surrounding the will, but Esther wrote a letter to her aunt later that year explaining that a friend had informed her husband that a will had been proved, but she was unwise as to the bequests it contained. In a reply, written by Mary Winn on 15 December, all was revealed. Upon reading of Esther's frustration, Mary had decided to go straight to Doctors' Commons, where she read the will herself, so that 'you might not be any longer kept in suspense of what it contained.' She continued:

> And very sorry I was to find she has left everything to your brother, never mentioning your name any other ways. But the reason she had disposed of all her effects in the manner she then had done was because you had married contrary to her approbation.

There was rather more to it than Mary had divulged. The crux of the matter concerned the precise wording of a will made by Sabine's mother, that is to say, Esther's Swiss maternal grandmother.

In 1779, Lady Sabine Winn's mother had revised her will, 'substituting' Sabine, her only heir, in place of Sabine's daughter Esther, who stood to inherit her grandparents' Swiss estates. But there was a condition. This condition reserved Sabine the right to 'deprive her [Esther] of the said substitution and to dispose thereof otherwise as she shall think fit, [if] our said granddaughter Winn should happen to marry against the liking and will of her mother.' In other words, Esther's grandmother left the entirety of her estates to Esther, unless, in her mother's opinion, she went off and married a wrong 'un. With that in mind, it's perhaps unsurprising to read this passage in Lady Sabine's will, which followed a direct citation from her mother's will:

> And whereas my said daughter hath married very imprudently and entirely against the liking and will of me her mother now by virtue of the right above writs to be reserved to me and by virtue of every other right power and authority vested in me I do hereby deprive her of the benefit of the said substitution and do give devise and bequeath the same and also all other my real and personal estate whatsoever and wheresoever and of

what nature or kindsoever both in England and Switzerland or elsewhere subject nevertheless and charged and chargeable with the payment of all my just debts unto my dear son Sir Rowland Winn Baronet his heirs executors and administrators to hold and to the use of him my said son his heirs executors administrators and assigns forever.

On proving the will, Sir Rowland killed off any hopes his sister had of inheriting her mother's or indeed her grandmother's estates, an inheritance Esther was presumably aware of and expecting to receive on her mother's death. Mary explained that Mr Watson had prepared the will (she detested the man and couldn't resist stirring up trouble when opportunities presented themselves). So what words of advice could Esther's sage aunt offer her now? Was it to cut her ties with Nostell once and for all and bring an end to relations with her brother, who had failed to consider her feelings, had kept her in the dark about their mother's death and then tried to hide the existence of the will? No, of course not! Instead, Mary's attention turned once more to the diamonds that had once belonged to Esther's grandmother.

Write to Sir Rowland, Mary urged, but exclusively about the stones. And if she heard nothing in six weeks' time, then Mary suggested it would be time for Esther's husband to engage a lawyer to try to wrest them from her brother, 'for have them I would, they are your own, and positively he should not keep them.' Nor, she said, should Sir Rowland 'keep your ten thousand pounds in his hands' (the sum that was due to Esther owing to a clause in her parents' marriage settlement).

Mary told her niece not to send any more letters to Mr Watson, 'which I think you were wrong in doing before, knowing he is no friend of yours, and perhaps might never have informed your brother of it.' She also felt that Esther's husband should exert himself, otherwise 'he will be trod upon, and why should you be starving when you have sufficient of your own to prevent it.' Mary wished she lived nearer to Esther so that she might 'spur up your husband, for I know none of your family will blame him for it, but rather commend him, so don't be afraid.'

The comment about Esther starving was seemingly in response to the last letter she had written to her aunt when she'd apparently explained that the smallholding her family lived on was not proving a success.

As it happened, Esther had already decided to make her own enquiries with Doctors' Commons, and had received a reply before her aunt had written to spill the beans. In a letter Esther wrote to Mr Watson, penned four days prior to Mary's, she expressed her frustration at the situation:

> I received your favour of the 2nd instant (concerning the will) for which I thank you. I had just received one from the Doctors' Commons, for having heard so many different reports I was determined to be satisfied respecting it, but however I find the whole has been nothing more than tales, spread abroad by malicious persons in order to tantalize me. I must confess I was rather hurt when I came to look over the will, to find that my mother had not the humanity to make me even the most trifling recompense for the many years that I most faithfully attended on her, nor to give orders for the giving up of several things which she had in her possession of which I have every right and title to.

Esther's wish list

Esther reminded Mr Watson that some years earlier she had sent him a list of possessions she wished to have sent to her, and that Watson, having presented this to her mother, had told Esther that some of these would indeed be returned, but, she reminded him, none ever were. 'I had some thoughts of coming over,' Esther continued, and no doubt referring to her uncle, Sir George Strickland, she added, 'and there is a person of some consequence in the neighbourhood that offered to accompany me.' But she told Mr Watson that as he'd been so kind to offer to present her list to her brother, she would hold off visiting. Esther explained that she certainly didn't want to have 'any litigation with my brother, neither should I wish to give the least mortification, which coming to him on such an occasion might cause.' Then followed a list of the articles that Esther wanted her brother to send to Morton:

> [First], the jewels, left me by my grandmother when sent down to Nostell by Sir Joshua Vannock, in whose care they were, [which] were in a small ornamented casket, and as near as I can recollect, consisted of a diamond necklace; earrings; an ornament for the hair; 3 or 4 rings, some I believe set ones; and a pair of

ruby earrings. I think there perhaps may be some other articles, but as I only saw them once, or twice, at most, I cannot exactly ascertain.

Second, a large gold double cased repeater, the outward case embossed with a gold face. It was my grandmother's and when given [to] me it had a twisted gold ladies' chain with some trinkets which I cannot now exactly describe.

Third, a small gold watch, which my father brought from Switzerland and gave me. The case was figured or carved and ornamented with different coloured gold.

Fourth, there were 3 or 4 boxes or caskets containing various trinkets, coins &c. in a mahogany piece of furniture with doors and drawers underneath that stood in what was called 'my room', which you may remember, I delivered up the keys for, along with some others … as some of the drawers contained a quantity of Swiss lace and other things which I did not wish to claim during my mother's life, although they had been given to me.

Esther wrote that she'd always lived in hope that 'some happy event' would lead to reconciliation with her mother, 'before death parted us'. But it was not to be: 'my mother, at that trying hour still held me in the same contempt.' She then described some paintings she wished to be returned to her, 'if they are still in being.' She described these as:

Two pictures which my mother gave me that came from abroad: one a cattle piece in an old fashioned gilt frame, the other [depicting] horses, one a skewbald, this without a frame. They were in a small room on the best stair case, next to what was called the red and yellow room, and the next door but one to the room in which you [her brother] slept. Though perhaps my mother might [have] since removed them into the room where Sir Thomas More's picture was, as several were carried there before I left Nostell.

'Sir Thomas More's picture' refers to a copy of a now lost Hans Holbein painting by Elizabethan artist Rowland Lockey. It shows Sir Thomas More, the statesman, Lord High Chancellor and councillor to Henry VIII, sitting with his family, and is aptly known by the name *Sir Thomas More and his family*. The painting, commissioned by More's son, Thomas, which is still hanging at Nostell Priory today, was long thought to be Holbein's own, whose sketch for the original painting appears below. The Nostell version was later shown to have been a copy: the presence on the painting of Lockey's signature, 'Rolandus Lockey', and the year 1592, given Holbein died in 1543, being something of a giveaway. It had come into the Winn family as part of a marriage dowry when the 4th Baronet married Susanna Henshaw, whose ancestor, Margaret Roper, was the daughter of Sir Thomas More. This lady is shown in the sketch sitting in the foreground holding a book.

Esther also hoped her brother might let her have a piano, 'which stands in the yellow dining room.' She wasn't sure whether she had any claim on the instrument but it was of sentimental value to her, having learned to play on it as a young girl. And she didn't think Sir Rowland would miss it, 'he having one so far superior.' If he wasn't prepared to hand it over, Esther was

Holbein's sketch of the painting copied by Rowland Lockey, which hangs in the Lower Hall at Nostell Priory. From *Hans Holbein the Younger*, by Arthur Bensley Chamberlain.

prepared to pay for it. She ended by telling Mr Watson that 'any impartial person' would see that her brother had 'great reasons to make me some little returns for the favours I have shewn him'. Esther pointed out that she had lost the opportunity of earning interest on the money due to her from her father's estate as so much of it had been kept back when it was due. She pointed out that losing such sums 'is very considerable' bearing in mind how small her present income was, but trusted she was not wrong in her opinion of her brother, who she hoped would not want to see her 'a loser'.

Shepley Watson endorsed the letter, explaining that he had answered it per Sir Rowland's directions, who 'wished to do everything that was right' but unfortunately, 'had no recollection of the particulars of the things himself; or of what passed between his mother and herself [Esther].' Watson wrote that Sir Rowland had not yet looked in any of his mother's rooms since her death (fifteen months earlier), 'but that when he does I am to accompany him and he means to do what is perfectly right.' Watson did enclose an account of the interest due to Esther, which amounted to £250.

The following year, 1800, was for Esther an *annus horribilis*. In April her friend and confidant Mary Winn passed away in her sixties, leaving a £20 bequest to Esther in a will dated December 1797, written just a few months after their correspondence had begun. Then disaster struck.

On 22 May 1800, Esther's beloved husband John died, aged just thirty-three. Esther was heartbroken. In a draft letter to a 'dear friend', Miss Grundy, she wrote of a 'heavy calamity' that had befallen her, explaining that she'd 'lost my all; my only comfort in this world.' As far as she was concerned there was no happiness left to her 'on this side of the grave', adding, 'I have nothing to do but to prepare myself that I may be worthy to join him in that world when we shall be no more separated.' Esther and John had hoped that the poor health he'd suffered in Manchester would be improved in the Lincolnshire countryside, this, according to Esther, being 'his native air', the letter thus revealing that if he had been Nostell's baker, he wasn't a local man. In the April John had complained of feeling weaker than ever and told Esther he didn't expect to see the summer. Despite Esther's prayers 'daily, I may say hourly … to the supreme almighty orderer of all things, that it would please him to spare to me yet a few years, so dear and valuable a friend,' John's condition worsened, and at the beginning of May he grew 'very thin indeed'. Esther described a slow fever, constant thirst, shudders, jaundice, and a weakness that confined her husband to bed. She remained hopeful of his recovery but was told by a doctor that her husband was suffering from consumption. He prescribed medicine that at first seemed to revive John, and Esther thought 'all the danger was over', but it was a temporary reprieve and soon the doctor made it quite clear that 'all hopes were over.' Esther wanted to keep this terrible fate from John but he knew the end approached, actually telling her, 'I know all is over with me.' Despite his speech having all but failed about an hour before he died, Esther did hear him mutter 'happy, happy Lord' as he said his final prayers, and then, at twelve thirty, 'he departed this life and went to join our two little angels that were gone before'. Esther had lost a 'tender husband and a faithful companion to all who knew him'.

An interesting snapshot of the simpler, plainer life Esther enjoyed at Morton with her husband, away from the grand pile at Nostell, with all its trappings, is illustrated by the inventory of his goods and chattels, made not long after his death. Firstly, John had died possessing £77 of 'ready money and security for money' and £30 worth of plate, linen and wearing apparel. In the 'little parlour' there were two tables, a secretary desk, and a bookcase, which were valued at £14 11s. The Williamsons' 'best low front room' contained a pianoforte (probably not the one at Nostell that Esther had hoped to be reunited with), chairs and a sofa worth £41 15s. A basic kitchen comprised a dresser, chairs, and fire irons, said to be worth £4 15s. There was a clock worth £4 in the passage, and in the 'first front chamber' stood a simple camp bed and crib, which would be expected to fetch £7 18s if offered for sale. The 'second front chamber' fared better, containing a bed and some drawers worth £20 12s 6d. A back chamber, comprising a camp bed and more drawers worth £9 13s, completed the contents of the main house, save for the carpet lying in the passage, valued at £2. A small bed and a tool box, valued at £1 18s, could be found in the 'first front garret', and there was a cart and a ladder in the courtyard worth £5. A dairy churn, some pots, and tubs and a cheese press in the brewhouse added £2 to the value of the estate. Then, with specific reference to the Williamsons' smallholding, the inventory appraisers valued a haystack at £10, Galloway cattle at £5 5s, two cows at £16, two calves at £5 and two pigs at £1, which meant John's whole estate amounted to no more than £258 7s 6d – not bad for a baker/smallholder but peanuts to the likes of the Nostell baronets.

Four days after his death, John was buried at St Peter's Church in Scotter, not far from Morton. A gravestone was inscribed 'Sacred to the memory of John Williamson of Morton, Gent: near Gainsborough, who departed this life on the 22 May 1800, aged 33 years.'

Later that year, Esther received a letter from an old acquaintance from Manchester, Mrs Gould of Lees House, Ardwick Green. She was well aware of Esther's trials and tribulations, and was evidently responding to a letter she'd had from Esther, presumably informing Mrs Gould of John's demise. The pair had parted on bad terms when Esther and John had moved to Lincolnshire, Mrs Gould writing:

I said some things to you at our parting which I wish you would remember. I would have said more, but my heart was so deeply concerned, and so very sincere, that I found my emotion too great, which obliged me to turn from you in haste, and though I thought you spoke to me, I could not without pain turn to you again.

Now she wrote to offer further advice to her old friend, who she feared would end up the object of the desires of many of a bounty hunter, given the fortune still due to Esther from her brother, who'd paid small amounts of his sister's money with great reluctance. Mrs Gould wrote:

Think of your sufferings in child bearing and your faintings after your last was borne. You have once you know acted against the advice of those nearest related to you. I am convinced you must at times have had painful reflections. O my dear Mrs W, there is but one fit plan for you now to pursue: that is to be determined to regain your brother's love and put yourself under his protection and take pleasure in him and your children. Your fortune will now be the greatest object for men to hunt after. On that account you will have many offers, but mind what I say. It will not be by those who have £500 a year. If a Lady was to say that her brother had only paid her money out of goodwill for her support, but that if she married a second time, he would not give a shilling and he had let her know as much and that whoever took her would have her and her children to support, this would soon prove to any woman what a man's view was.

Clearly warming to her to theme, Mrs Gould kept going, firmly blaming Esther's present situation on her choice of 'acquaintance'. 'My dear,' she proclaimed, 'you are the daughter of a Baronet and of a Lady, your brother a man of the same rank. Why should you sink so much below your natural right in society?' Failing to consider the small matter of Esther's ill-treatment at Nostell and her immense love for her late husband, the all-knowing correspondent had much more to say. She felt Esther should 'quit [her] present situation' for 'that might lead to a friendship with [her] brother.' Mrs Gould also wished Esther would write to her often, consult her and take her advice, plainly not wanting to lose a good source of gossip. And to ensure nothing rebounded her way, she also begged Esther not to 'name to anyone what I say for your good.' She even offered to write to Sir Rowland on Esther's behalf and then imparted some parenting advice with regard to one of Esther's sons who was causing his mother a few headaches.

> And pray whip that little boy well and keep his spirit under when he is young and he will be both a better and a more dutiful son. But I see if he is not corrected now, he will soon be too old and too headstrong and may be to you the cause of great grief. Your very best plan with him would be to send him now to a good master. He should not remain longer with you. He is quite old enough. He finds he can do anything with you, with his tormenting, teasing way. But pray, break him of it.

Mrs Gould finished her letter by informing Esther that she was not formed for 'great trials, and hardships', advised her not to 'risk her future happy state', and wished her well.

As it turned out, a new man did enter Esther's life. On 25 July 1801 at the church of St Mary-le-Wigford, in Lincoln, following the granting of a licence from the Archdeaconry of Lincoln, she married a second time, and coincidentally and confusingly, her new groom was also called John Williamson, a local gentleman.

A marriage settlement was drawn up on the day of their marriage, which, once and for all, confirmed that Esther's first husband had indeed been a baker.

This new marriage was not a happy one, Christopher Todd describing it as 'disastrous'. The pair separated a year later and sixteen months after

St Mary-le-Wigford, next to Lincoln Central railway station.

that, on 6 December 1803, at the age of just thirty-three, Esther passed away. On 23 December, she was buried at Scotter beside her first husband, bringing about a tragic end to a tormented life.

Esther's heirs

But there was to be a twist. Esther's brother, the young baronet, who Dr Wright described in his *Reminiscences* as a 'gay fox-hunter, chiefly taking pleasure, as I was told, in his hounds and horses', died from consumption in October 1805 at Nostell, at the age of just thirty, outliving his mother by only seven years. He was intestate, unmarried and without issue. So whilst Lady Sabine Winn had comprehensively disinherited Esther in favour of her son, the 6th Baronet, his heirs were none other than Esther and John Williamson's three children, John, Charles and Louisa. Following their mother's death, the trio had been welcomed to Nostell by the late baronet, who had appointed Mary's and Esther's nemesis, Shepley Watson, as their guardian.

But with the death of the 6th Baronet, the Nostell baronetcy (but crucially not the entailed house) went to a distant cousin, Mark Edmund Winn of Ackton. The house, though, was inherited by John Williamson, Esther's eldest son, and in 1815, upon turning twenty-one, he changed his name to Winn, as recorded in one of Shepley Watson's account books.

> On 27 March 1815 Mr Williamson attained his age of 21 years; and the Prince Regent has granted to him His Majesty's Royal License and authority (dated 27th Feb 1815) to assume the surname and bear the arms of Winn only.

Tragically, John Winn, formerly Williamson, died from consumption (just as his father had) while touring Rome in 1817, aged just twenty-three, and without issue. That meant his brother, Charles, now inherited the Nostell estate. Charles and his sister Louisa, following their late brother's lead, duly changed their names to Winn on 17 February 1818. The following year,

A sketch of Nostell Priory by George S. Elgood, from *A Picturesque History of Yorkshire*, by J.S. Fletcher.

on 14 June, at St Andrew's Church, Boynton, Charles married his second cousin, Priscilla Strickland, the great-granddaughter of the 4th Baronet. This union effectively allowed the Winns to step back in time to more harmonious days, or as Christopher Todd put it, 'it was as if the family were closing ranks after an intrusion by a foreigner ... it is tempting to see the final consecration of the reunion of sides of the family who had quarreled during Sabine's lifetime.'

Our old friend Catherine Cappe certainly approved of the match. In a letter written to Priscilla's mother, Lady Strickland of Boynton, sent on hearing of the couple's engagement, she had this to say:

> Many thanks for your friendly communication ... respecting the intended connection between the houses of Boynton and Nostell. Most sincerely do I wish the two young people all the happiness they can reasonably expect and that they may long be examples to many others of every Christian virtue. It is a connection in which I am persuaded, my good friend, their excellent and most highly respected great-grandfather would have truly respected, and sincerely do I hope it may lead to the removal of that moral cloud which unhappily so long obscured the prosperity and happiness of a family, which, in the days of other times, was so justly and honourably distinguishable.

Charles Winn's impact on Nostell Priory was significant. He'd been educated at Emmanuel College at the University of Cambridge, where he matriculated in 1815, and on graduating, he evidently entered the clergy. In her essay *A cultivated eye for the antique*, published in the visual arts magazine *Apollo* in April 2003, Sophie Raikes confirmed that Charles took holy orders, and indeed he was recorded as the incumbent of the parish church at Wragby in 1829. In 1825, he began restoring the church, work that he completed a decade later. He added furniture, including a Norman font rescued from a chapel in the abandoned East Yorkshire coastal village of Auburn, and a Venetian pulpit, and fabulous stained glass from Switzerland dating back to the 1500s. An inscription in the oak panelled vestry at Wragby reads: *Hoc sacrarium Carolo Winn armigero ornatum est Annon Domini MDCCCXXVII.* The church also contains the Winn Chapel, commissioned by Charles

IN THE VAULT BENEATH LIES INTERRED THE BODY OF
JOHN WINN, OF NOSTELL PRIORY, ESQUIRE,
WHO DEPARTED THIS LIFE AT HOME THE 6TH DAY OF NOVEMBER A.D. 1817,
IN THE 21ST YEAR OF HIS AGE.
THIS MONUMENT WAS ERECTED BY CHARLES AND LOUISA WINN,
AS A TRIBUTE OF RESPECT TO THE MEMORY OF
A BELOVED AND AFFECTIONATE BROTHER,
A.D. 1826.

The memorial to John Winn.

and Louisa and dedicated to the memory of their brother, John. Shields were added later to mark the deaths of Charles and Louisa.

During his tenure, Charles, a prolific diarist, also oversaw the completion and reimagining of several of the rooms at Nostell that had been left unfinished following his grandfather's death in 1785 and a lack of action on his uncle's part. A 'Plan of the House' drawn by Jean Godwin and published in Maurice Brockwell's *Nostell Collection*, shows, for example, the Tapestry Room, a room designed by Robert Adam but which Charles was responsible for completing. From 1819 to 1836, Charles employed London interior decorator Thomas Ward, of 67 Frith Street, Soho Square, to repaint several of Adam's rooms and also to supply furniture and curtains. These changes were the last substantial alterations made at Nostell, the house otherwise remaining fairly faithful to the original eighteenth-century vision.

But, home improvements aside, it was his love of collecting antiques, books and paintings for which Charles Winn is perhaps best remembered. Many of the titles in the Nostell Library were purchased by Charles and he acquired paintings by old masters such as Rembrandt, Van Dyck, Gainsborough, Hogarth et al., and portraits of characters from the Tudor court, though it was later discovered some of the old master paintings were actually copies.

Charles also enjoyed amassing curios, one of which was a double-barrelled flintlock gun said to belong to Napoleon, which rests on the Chippendale desk in the Library in the image shown earlier.

In 1838, the bibliographer Thomas Frognall Dibdin published the first volume of his *Bibliographical Antiquarian and Picturesque Tour of the Northern Counties of England and in Scotland*. One of the stops on this impressive tour was the ancient town of Wakefield, where Dibdin was met by his friend the Reverend Samuel Sharp, the vicar of Wakefield. Reverend Sharp was 'most anxious' that Dibdin 'should take [the] first opportunity of paying [his] respects at Nostel Priory, the seat of Charles Winn, Esq.' Dibdin was keen to visit the priory, not least because he wanted to see the painting of Thomas More, which, he wrote, he had 'panted almost thirty years to see'. But he'd also heard of Mr Winn's 'gentlemanly courteousness and hospitality' and the house, the grounds and the church all 'contributed amazingly to whet my appetite and accelerate my movements.'

Dibdin was not disappointed by what he found and described receiving a warm reception when he arrived, unannounced and uninvited.

It is a large and noble mansion, with a grand flight of steps, unsecured by a balustrade. We entered the lower, or ground apartments; and saw servants and children flitting in all directions. This could not be the abode of melancholy. Two large wooden seats, or sofas, of the time of Elizabeth or James, shewed the owner to have an eye of taste in matters of ancient furniture. We ascended, perhaps abruptly: but there was no helping it. Mr Winn made his appearance, and in a trice I was introduced to my dear old acquaintance, Sir Thomas More. I might be said, for a little moment, to have silently worshipped the picture. Its entirety and freshness surpassed all expectation.

Dibdin marvelled at the painting, believing that, perhaps, there was no more precious a piece of art in the whole of England. But something niggled away at him. He couldn't dispel the feeling that this wasn't the original Holbein painting, which of course, it isn't. He also felt it belonged in the National Gallery, and then went on to imagine two national galleries. A second gallery, he thought, ought to house historical portraits 'who forever live upon the canvas of history. Who would not wish to see some three hundred feet of wall covered, as well as animated, by such a pictorial display?' He was clearly a man ahead of his time; the National Portrait Gallery did not open in its original location on Great George Street, Westminster until 15 January 1859, some twenty-one years after Dibdin's visit to Nostell. After marvelling at the painting, Dibdin, who was travelling with his daughter, was conveyed 'to a delightful drawing-room, connected with a music-room of dimensions sufficiently ample for the notes of an organ, and the human voice, to reach all ears and move all hearts'.

They were then shown around Nostell's other rooms, enjoying the views from certain windows, and then to the church, where Dibdin was much impressed by such a neat, compact, beautiful edifice. His only regret was the lack of stained glass. 'Wait a while,' Charles Winn told him. 'When I was abroad I purchased sufficient stained glass to fill the interstices of every mullion in the church. Be easy on this score.' Dibdin was relieved that the church, which had recently been repaired, was in good hands, with Charles Winn as its patron, writing:

> not only that the patron of the living, and proprietor of the church, had a cultivated eye for the antique, in matters of furniture, but a cultivated heart to spare no pains, and lose no opportunity, of possessing himself of a good thing.

It was also during Charles's time that coal mining, a pursuit carried on at Nostell by the original hermits of so many centuries ago, was increased on the Winn estates. A new pit was sunk in Wragby village in the 1830s. In his illuminating postdoctoral thesis, *Coal Mining on a Yorkshire Estate*, David Stewart Cross wrote that this pit 'raised 10–15,000 tons' per annum, which he calculated brought only a very modest addition to the family income. It was the discovery in the late 1850s of ironstone on their Lincolnshire estates, which, along with Nostell coal, allowed the Winns to make steel. It was these enterprises together that elevated the financial position of the family, following something of a monetary crisis earlier that decade.

In 1866, another Winn colliery was opened, the aptly named Nostell Colliery, which had been sunk from 1864 to 1866. It was managed by the Winn family and its location, by the new Nostell railway station, was advantageous, as was its timing. The West Riding and Grimsby Joint Railway had also begun in 1866, and with Nostell as one of its stops, it provided the Great Northern Railway with a new line from Doncaster to Wakefield, both major stations on the national network with services to London, allowing easy transportation of the Nostell coal to an expanding client base. The colliery, which was run by the family until 1918 (when it became a private limited company), got off to a steady start, eventually returning a healthy profit, and by 1896 it was producing over 200,000 tonnes of coal annually. Operations continued for the best part of the next century, until production was halted in 1987, and along with so many of the nation's collieries that decade, it was closed forever. Housing for the colliers and their families had been provided on a long street called Nostell Row, also known as Long Row. But typically conditions were unsanitary, an issue not properly addressed until the late 1890s when a drain was added so that water could be drained from the 'row'. Soon after the houses were erected, Charles Winn, realizing there was a need to educate the colliers' children, had funded the building of a school.

Nostell Colliery.

Nostell Station.

Charles died on 17 December 1874. The *Yorkshire Post and Leeds Intelligencer*, one of several provincial newspapers to report his death the following day, had this to say:

DEATH OF MR CHARLES WINN, OF PONTEFRACT

The announcement of the death of Mr Charles Winn, of Nostell Priory, near Pontefract, at the advanced age of 79 years, will be received with deep regret. The deceased gentleman's character as a public man in the country is well known. Mr Winn had been under the advice of Dr Grabham, of Pontefract, for several years past, but had up to within a few days ago been in his usual moderate health, when he was severely attached with bronchitis, and combined with the inclement season, his aged frame was unable to bear up against its weight, and he died last night about seven o'clock.

He was succeeded by his son and heir, Conservative MP Rowland Winn, who would be created the first Baron St Oswald in 1885.

If only Esther had lived to see at least some of her son's successes.

Chapter 5

Nostell in the News

During the nineteenth century, the increasing number of provincial newspapers appearing in Britain regularly reported news from Nostell, interest in the family and the goings on at the house stretching well beyond Yorkshire's borders. Through the following extracts, a selection of remarkable incidents and, perhaps, little-known events from that century are described.

Globe, Tuesday, 20 January 1818
FUNERAL OF JOHN WINN, ESQ.

On Tuesday last the remains of John Winn, Esq. of Nostell, Yorkshire, nephew and heir of the late Sir Rowland Winn, Bart. were deposited in the family vault in Wragby Church. Mr Winn died at Rome, on the 17th November last. The corpse was conveyed over-land to Calais, was landed at Dover, on the 22nd December, attended by Dr Harrison, who had accompanied him as his friend and physician on his tour on the Continent and by his valet, &c. and arrived at the family mansion at Nostell, on the 6th inst. The funeral was very numerously and respectably attended. About two o'clock in the afternoon, the procession moved from the house to the church in the following order:

The Undertakers
Thirty-four Tenants in Scarfs
Mules two and two
A Hearse, conveying the Corpse, in a Coffin, covered with black velvet, and richly ornamented with a silver engraved plate and nails.
Chief Mourners – Mr and Miss Williamson, Brother and Sister of the Deceased, and two other Gentleman, Relatives of the Family, in a Coach:
Six Gentlemen, Pall-bearers, in another.

In other carriages were Sir Francis Lindley Wood, Bart. and his son; Godfrey Wentworth Wentworth, Esq. and his eldest son; Colonel Cholmley, Shepley Watson, Esq., Mrs. Watson, &c. &c.

The procession was closed by Mr Winn's carriage, and two others empty, followed by his valet, house-steward, domestic servants, and tradesmen.

A large concourse of people assembled to witness the solemn scene, of a young man, the recent inheritor of the estates and fortunes of an ancient and splendid family, early conveyed to the narrow house appointed for all living. The solemn service was read on this mournful occasion by the Rev John Griffiths, of Emmanuel College, Cambridge, his friend and tutor. Mr Winn was twenty-three years of age, and promised to be an honourable and respectable representative of the House of Winn. His extensive estates descend to his only surviving brother, Charles Williamson, Esq. a fellow-commoner of Emmanuel College, Cambridge, and now in his twenty-second year.

The remains of the deceased were enclosed in three coffins, the shell and exterior one of wood, the middle one of lead. These were formed according to the custom of Italy, nearly in the shape of a wedge, and after the arrival of the corpse at Nostell another was put over them of the English shape, which was in consequence obliged to be made unusually large, being eight feet four inches long, and three feet broad.

Yorkshire Gazette, Saturday, 19 June 1819
Marriages
On Wednesday last, at Boynton, Charles Winn, Esq. of Nostell Priory, to Priscilla, youngest daughter of Sir W. Strickland, Bart.

This marriage notice refers to Nostell by its present name, Nostell Priory, which is thought to have come into use during Charles's time, he being a keen antiquarian.

Leeds Intelligencer, Monday, 28 February 1820
Births
On Saturday week, the Lady of Charles Winn, Esq. of Nostel Priory, in this county, of a son and heir.

Rowland Winn was born 19 February 1820. He became the first Baron St Oswald in 1885.

Yorkshire Gazette, Saturday 11 October 1823

Zebu – A small herd of this singular description of animals, consisting of a bull and several cows and calves, passed through this town on Friday last for the park of C. Winn, Esq. at Nostell.

Yorkshire Gazette, Saturday 1 April 1826
YORKSHIRE LENT ASSIZES, CRIMINAL COURT – Before
Mr Baron Hullock, MONDAY, March 27

John Darley (31) & Thomas Allen (32), for a misdemeanour.

This was an offence under the game laws. It is a transportable offence to be found in a plantation at night armed, with an intent to kill game; and the prisoners were charged with being in the grounds of Charles Winn, Esq. of Nostel, on the night of the 27th December last, with the above intent. The evidence was not however sufficient to convict them; and they were accordingly ACQUITTED.

Leeds Intelligencer, Thursday 12 July 1827

On Tuesday week, Charles Winn, Esq. of Nostel, held his half-yearly rent-day, for his farming tenants; when, after dinner, he generously returned to each of them 10 per cent upon the money they had just paid. It is almost unnecessary to say, that, highly pleased with this unexpected bounty of their landlord, the whole tenantry drank his health and that of his family, with enthusiastic applause.

Leeds Intelligencer, Thursday, 12 August 1830
YORKSHIRE HORTICULTURE SOCIETY

The first August Meeting of this Society took place on the 3d instant, at the Music Saloon, Wakefield.

A new variety of melon, raised from seed obtained in Persia, was exhibited by the gardener of C. Winn, Esq. of Nostell Priory. It is called the *Keising Melon*, and was much admired.

Yorkshire Gazette, Saturday, 7 May 1831
ELECTION INTELLIGENCE
Beverley Election

On Saturday, the election of two representatives for the town of Beverley took place. The candidates first in the field were Mr Burton, of Hotham Hall; and Mr Wm Marshall, son of John Marshall, Esq. of Leeds. Mr Burton was understood to be favourable to the reform bill of ministers, with the exception of that clause which goes to deprive the descendants of freemen of the elective franchise; and Mr Marshall to be a stickler for the whole bill. The friends of both parties were actively employed during the week in strengthening their several interests amongst the burgesses, in the event of any opposition arising. Mr Lane Fox, who had been applied to by the third or pink party, who last election voted in favour of Mr Capel Cure, was understood to have declined, and even so late as Friday afternoon all ideas of a contest seemed to have been abandoned. On Friday, however, most unexpectedly by the inhabitants of the town, a third man was announced, in the person of Charles Winn, Esq. of Nostel Priory, who came forward as an independent country gentlemen, unconnected with any party; desirous only for the stability, honour, and prosperity of the country. He declared himself friendly to measures of reform, so far as admitting to a participation of the elective franchise, those interests which have grown into importance by wealth and industry; while on the other hand, he pledged himself to watch narrowly those schemes of change which evidently tend to the subversion of the church and state. His first study would be to protect the just rights and privileges of freemen, but never to diminish them; and therefore, he would do all his power to prevent those, who, by birth or servitude, have acquired a voice in the representation, from being unjustly deprived of handing down that right to their posterity. He declared himself opposed to slavery, in every part of the world, and in the disposal of the public purse, his efforts should always be directed to the economy.

When polling closed, Marshall received 731 votes, Burton 707 votes and Charles Winn, in last place, 349 votes. He stood for the same seat again in 1832 and once more found himself in last place.

Leeds Times, Saturday, 31 August 1833

FIRE – About noon last Sunday, a hay-stack in the farm-yard of Chas. Winn, Esq. of Nostel Priory, was discovered to be on fire: information was immediately dispatched to Wakefield, and Mr Wild, of Kirkgate, with the Leeds and Yorkshire Company's engine, was on the spot within eighteen minutes after the intelligence reached him; which, considering the distance (almost six miles), was a surprising exertion. The engine belonging to the premises had, however, nearly succeeded in extinguishing the fire before any serious damage was sustained.

Sheffield Independent, Saturday, 18 February 1837
SUICIDE AT NOSTEL

About nine o'clock on Saturday morning last, a labouring man whilst going to his work, perceived a woman throw herself into the lake at Nostel Priory. He immediately called out for assistance and having procured further aid, took the boat and began to grapple for the body. The first thing they took out of the water was the poor woman's apron, which she wrapped round her face before she jumped into the water. They next brought up the cloak, and at length succeeded in dragging out the unfortunate woman, who, life not being quite extinct, gave two or three slight sobs; but notwithstanding the efforts made for her recovery, all proved unavailing. It appeared on subsequent inquiry, that the deceased, who was about forty years of age, was cook at Mr Magnay's, the White Hart Inn, Wakefield, and that she had left there about seven the same morning, on a pretence of going to see her son, who she said resided at Nostel. The unfortunate woman had also been frequently heard to speak of the nice water at Nostel.

Yorkshire Gazette, Saturday, 17 February 1838
SERIOUS COACH ACCIDENT

On Saturday last, as the Doncaster and Wakefield Express coach was proceeding to the latter town, a serious accident occurred from the breaking of the axletree. Mr Abraham Lockwood, the coachman, who is one of the proprietors of the coach, was driving at a steady pace, and when between Wragby and Nostell, he heard a noise underneath the coach, and immediately pulled up the horses, and the coach fell over on the driver's side. The consequence was, that by the act of pulling up, Lockwood was thrown from his seat with great force, and his head coming in contact with a newly stoned part of the road, he was much bruised by the concussion, and was for some time quite insensible. Besides the bruises on his skull, the coach fell upon his legs, and he was much hurt on various parts of his body. He now lies in a dangerous state at his house in Wakefield. We are informed that Lockwood had full command of his horses at the time of the accident, and that had he not fortunately pulled up at the precise moment, the probability is that some lives would have been lost. As it was, he was himself the greatest sufferer. Some of the passengers were slightly injured, and others escaped with no further harm than fright. Mrs Winn, of Nostell Priory, on hearing of the accident, came immediately to the spot, with several attendants, and we have authority for stating that this lady's humane conduct was beyond all praise. Having attended personally to the coachman, Mrs Winn ordered one of the female passengers, a woman in a state of pregnancy, to be removed to Wragby, where the utmost attention was paid to her, and a message was sent to her husband at Wakefield, informing him of the circumstance, and of his wife's safety. The other passengers, after receiving the greatest kindness and attention from Mrs Winn, were forwarded by her orders to Wakefield in a carriage.

Yorkshire Gazette, Saturday, 15 January 1842
DEATHS
On Sunday, the 9th instant, at Nostell Priory, in this county, at the advanced age of 93 years, Sarah Mellard. She had lived in the service of the present Mr Winn and his predecessors for the unprecedented term of 83 years; and in the zealous and faithful discharge of her duty and gained the respect and esteem of the family.

Devizes and Wiltshire Gazette, Saturday, 7 January 1843
ANECDOTE OF OLD SIR ROWLAND WINN (reprinted from *Wakefield Journal*)
Not a century ago, there lived in Northgate, in this town [Wakefield], a fashionable staymaker, named Barber. Now in those days, this important part of a lady's dress was more stout and formidable than even at the

present time, indispensably requiring a 'try on' before it could be announced complete. One fine morning, Barber took horse and rode over to Nostell for that purpose. Meeting there with (as he supposed), a hanger-on about the house, he called out 'here my man – take care of my horse whilst I try a pair of stays on Lady Winn, and I will give you sixpence,' to which the man at once acceded. He then proceeded to the house where after concluding his errand, he was departing down the staircase when her ladyship accidentally approached the window just at the time and called out in great astonishment – 'Bless me, whose horse is Sir Rowland leading about?' The staymaker immediately perceiving his mistake, ran out and with many bows and scrapes, and a hundred apologies endeavoured to explain the matter. 'No, no,' said Sir Rowland, 'Mr Barber, you promised me sixpence, and as it is the first I ever earned in my life, I will have it.' The sixpence was then paid, and Barber departed glad to have escaped so easily.

Yorkshire Gazette, Saturday, 23 March 1844

JOHN DAVISON pleaded GUILTY to having on the 27 of January last, at Wragby, unlawfully married Jane Robson, his former wife being alive. The prisoner had been in the service of C. Winn, Esq. of Nostell Priory, along with Jane Robson, and whilst in that service had gained her affections and subsequently married her, he having a wife now alive. He was sentenced to be imprisoned for 18 calendar months to hard labour.

Leeds Intelligencer, Saturday, 19 January 1850
STEALING GAME

On Saturday last, Mr William Mason, landlord of the Boy and Barrel Inn, Market Place [Wakefield], was taken into custody on a charge of stealing a pheasant and a partridge, the property of Charles Winn, Esq., of Nostell Priory, under the following circumstances. It appeared that Mr Winn has an estate at Appleby, in Lincolnshire, from whence game has been frequently sent to Nostell during the last two years, and portions of which have several times been stolen whilst in transition between the two places. Various parties have been suspected, and Mr Winn at length communicated with Mr Macdonald, the chief constable of Wakefield, who laid a plan for the detection of the thief. A hamper of game was received at Wakefield Station, on Friday last, which was opened by Mr Macdonald, by whom all the birds were marked, and it was made up again and ultimately taken to the Boy and Barrel, where it remained all night, and was taken away on the following morning by the driver of the gig mail to Pontefract, by whom it was conveyed to Nostell. On being opened there by Mr Macdonald, a pheasant and partridge were found to be missing. On returning to Wakefield Mr Macdonald went to the house of Mason, who denied having any game in the house, but on Mr Macdonald's proceeding to search, he found the missing birds.

On the same day, the *Yorkshire Gazette* reported the death on 16 January of Priscilla Anne Winn, the daughter of Charles and Priscilla, at the age of just sixteen.

The case of William Mason was heard at Wakefield Sessions on 13 March 1850. He was acquitted by the jury following a sturdy defence

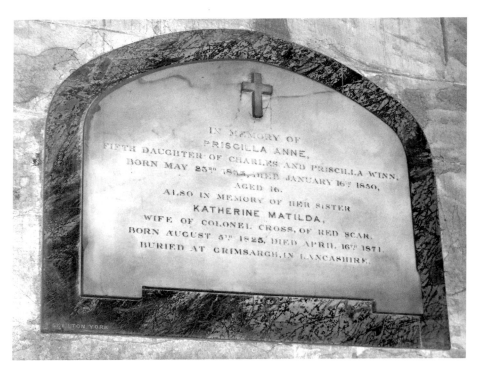

The memorial to Priscilla Anne Winn in the church at Wragby.

where it was suggested that somebody else might have removed the birds without Mason's knowledge and that charges of felony had previously been levelled at Macdonald himself, and thus he was not a reliable witness.

Liverpool Mercury, **Tuesday, 12 August 1851**

On Thursday evening week, a most distressing gig accident occurred near the Normanton station, by which the life of one individual has been sacrificed, and another person has been so seriously injured that great fears are entertained whether he will ultimately recover from the shock. The name of the unfortunate man who was killed is Frederick Bates, butler to Charles Winn, Esq., of Nostell Priory, near Wakefield, and the person who is injured is Mr Thorley, coachman to the above-named gentleman. The particulars of this distressing accident are as follows. On the evening above mentioned Mr Bates and Mr Thorley had been to the Normanton station with a friend in a gig, and they stayed a short time at the Commercial Inn, at Normanton, and then started with the intention of returning home to Nostell. Before leaving the Commercial Inn it was observed that the horse, which was a high spirited one, was getting unmanageable and plunged about very much. It seems that immediately after they had started the blinders slipped off, and the horse then ran away, and in turning a sharp corner the gig was upset, and the two occupants thrown out with great violence on the ground. Bates was so seriously injured that he died within three quarters of an hour after the accident occurred. Deceased, who was thirty-eight years of age, was a married man, and has a wife and four children at Liverpool. His remains were interred at Wragby church on Sunday afternoon last, and many a tear was shed at the melancholy end of one who merited the esteem and was so highly respected by all who knew him.

Frederick Bates was buried at Wragby on 3 August 1851, and the vicar, Robert Batty, appended a note to the entry in the parish register stating, 'Killed at Normanton 31 July 1851 by the upsetting of a dog-cart as he was returning from the station. REB.'

Morning Chronicle, **Thursday 23 March 1854**
Marriages

On the 21st inst., at St George's Hanover-square, Rowland Winn, Esq., eldest son of Charles Winn, Esq., of Nostell Priory, Yorkshire, and Appleby-hall, Lincolnshire, to Harriet Maria Amelia, second daughter of the late Lieutenant-Colonel Dumaresq, and niece of the Earl of Lanesborough.

Leeds Times, **Saturday, 18 December 1858**

On Thursday, before the West Riding magistrates, a respectable-looking woman, called Ann Bainbridge, was committed to the sessions on the charge of having stolen some drawers, petticoats, and other articles of wearing apparel, the property of one of the domestics at Nostell Priory. The apparel was in the drying ground belonging to the priory, and the loss was discovered on taking in the linen. Bainbridge having been seen in the Park, her house was searched, and in a box was found the missing linen all marked.

Sheffield Daily Telegraph, **Saturday, 8 January 1859**

ANN BAINBRIDGE, who had been out on bail, was charged with stealing at Nostell, on the 14th Dec., two chemise, the property of Mary Ann Steer; a chemise, two petticoats, two pairs of drawers, and other articles, the property of Ann Bandies; and also a nightgown, the property of Ann Rogerson. Guilty: two months.

Chelmsford Chronicle, **Friday 10 May 1861**
DEATH OF MISS WINN

On Thursday, the 25th ult., at Nostell Priory, Yorkshire, the seat of her brother, Charles Winn, Esq., aged 61, died Miss Louisa Winn. She was the only daughter of the late John Williamson, Esq., by Esther, only daughter of Sir Rowland Winn, fifth baronet, and sister of Sir Rowland Winn, sixth baronet, of Nostell Priory, who dying intestate and unmarried in 1805, the family estates passed to his nephew, the later John Williamson-Winn, Esq. (on whose death, in 1817, they were inherited by his brother, the present Charles Winn, Esq.,) while the baronetcy was merged in the superior title of Lord Headley.

Leeds Times, **Saturday 8 October 1864**

A frightful accident occurred at Nostell Colliery on Tuesday. A miner named John Hirst was engaged, along with a labourer, in taking down the props of a disused bank. As Hirst felled the fifth prop, a large stone, seven feet long, five feet broad, and twenty inches deep, dropped from the roof on the top of him, crushing him beneath it, and covering his head and shoulders completely, only leaving his legs free. Death must have been instantaneous. The stone was too large to be lifted, and it had to be broken before the body could be extricated. At the inquest, held on Wednesday, the jury returned a verdict of 'Accidentally crushed'.

Leeds Times, **Saturday 2 March 1867**

A fatal accident occurred on Saturday to the son of Mr George Nussey, at Nostell Colliery, near Pontefract. The youth, who was about thirteen years of age, was employed assisting to remove waggons from the screens to the sidings; whilst so engaged, he fell across the rails, and a waggon passed over both his legs, one of which it nearly severed from his body, and the other was so lacerated that both limbs had to be amputated. The poor youth did not long survive the operation. The jury, at the inquest, found a verdict of 'Accidental death'.

In November that same year, another youth, James Elliott, aged fifteen, a train driver at the colliery, also lost his life; the incident also ruled to be an accident. A further 'accident' occurred in February the following year when Henry Hargraves, a 40-year-old deputy at the colliery, was killed by a falling stone.

Lincolnshire Chronicle, **Friday, 11 December 1868**
OUR NEW MEMBERS OF PARLIAMENT

The Times published the following brief biographical notices of the new Members of the House of Commons. The Letters 'L' and 'C' distinguish the politics of each Member: [Liberal and Conservative].

WINN (North Lincolnshire) – Mr Rowland Winn (C), of Appleby Hall, Lincolnshire, is the eldest son of Mr Charles Winn, of Nostell Priory, Yorkshire, by Priscilla, daughter of the late Sir William Strickland. He was born in 1820, and was educated at Trinity College, Cambridge. He is a magistrate and deputy lieutenant for Lincolnshire, and for the East and West Ridings of Yorkshire. He married, in 1854, Harriet Maria Amelia, daughter of the late Colonel Henry and Lady Sophia Dumaresq, and niece of the late Earl of Lanesborough.

Rowland Winn remained Conservative Member of Parliament for North Lincolnshire until 1885, when he was raised to the peerage as Baron Saint Oswald of Nostell.

Leeds Mercury, Wednesday, 29 September 1869
A FISH POACHER DROWNED NEAR PONTEFRACT

On Monday afternoon a notorious poacher named James Lord, residing at Featherstone, near Pontefract, came to his death under the following circumstances. He and two others had been drinking at a public-house and had partaken of too much beer. They set off for a stroll from Wragby (it being the village feast) and went towards Foulby, near to which place a bridge crosses the lake belonging to Mr Winn, of Nostell Priory. The deceased looked over the bridge and saw a pike lying near the surface of the water, and foolishly jumped off the bridge to try to catch it, and was drowned in a few minutes in the presence of his companions. His body was shortly afterwards recovered and removed to Hill Top.

Pall Mall Gazette, Wednesday, 24 April 1872

Mr H. Strickland Constable, in a letter to *The Times*, states that on Wednesday, the 7th inst. about 6 PM, a stack of chimneys at Nostell Priory, the residence of Mr Charles Winn, was struck by lightning, which seems to have entered two contiguous chimneys, divided by a thin partition. This thin partition was untouched, but the stonework of each chimney, nearly a foot in thickness, was completely shattered and blown out, leaving a hole in each chimney nearly big enough for a wheelbarrow to enter. Stones bigger than a man's head were blown out horizontally, first over twenty-five feet of roof, and then over a flight of steps extending more than twenty feet from the wall of the house. Thus, they were thrown nearly fifty feet from the chimney into the carriage road below. A thunder-clap was heard at the same moment, like the report of a cannon. No trace of the electric fluid can be observed lower down in the chimney than the fracture described.

Leeds Times, Saturday, 17 June 1876
ROBBERY FROM NOSTELL PRIORY

At the Wakefield Court House, on Wednesday, a labourer named William Allen was charged with stealing a cash box and £150 in Bank of England notes, the property of Mr Charles Winn, of Nostell Priory. On the evening of Monday, the 12th of March 1872, some person entered a drawing-room at the Priory, and took away the money. As a labourer was proceeding to his work next morning, he found the cash-box near the park walls. The money was gone, but a number of papers were left behind. Subsequently the notes were traced to the possession of the prisoner, but before he could be apprehended he left the country. Recently he returned to England, and last Saturday he was taken into custody by an inspector connected with the Derbyshire constabulary. On the application of Detective Stansfield, of Leeds, the prisoner was remanded in custody for a week.

Ossett Observer, Saturday, 1 July 1876
THE ROBBERY FROM NOSTELL PRIORY IN 1872

On Saturday at the West Riding Sessions, Pontefract, before Mr W. Pell (chairman), Mr L. Jaques, Mr W.F. Tempest, and Mr T. Peel, the prisoner, William Allen, of Burton-on-Trent, in custody on the charge of entering Nostell Priory, and stealing a cashbox containing about £142 in bank notes and gold and silver coin, the property of Miss Caroline Sophia Winn, on the night of the 12th March 1872, was again brought up for examination. Miss Caroline Sophia Winn; Mrs Mary Dickenson, upper housemaid at Nostell Priory at the time of the robbery; John Greenfield, labourer; Mr F.H. Hennicker, clerk with Messrs Smith, Payne, and Smith, bankers, London; Mr Thos. Whitemore, Leeds; Henry Slinger, of the West Riding Prison; Mr F.W. Greabes, clerk in the Derby and Derbyshire Bank, having been examined in tracing the passage of the stolen notes from hand to hand, Inspector George Taylor, of the Derbyshire Constabulary, stated that on the 9th June he saw the prisoner at Derby, and charged him with robbery. Prisoner made a statement to witness, and described the circumstances of the robbery to the effect that having got into Nostell Park he found himself near the hall. Seeing a window open he entered. He afterwards went to Dewsbury, and then booked for Manchester, and thence to Derby, ultimately returning to Manchester, and then to Chester and Birkenhead, subsequently sailing in the *City of China* for New York. His statement showed that he returned to England some time ago, and had been working for several months at Messrs Whitworth's in Manchester. The bench committed the prisoner for trial at the Bradford Sessions.

Sheffield Independent, **Thursday, 28 September 1876**
Yesterday afternoon a demonstration of the South West Riding Union of Conservative Associations was held at Nostell Priory, near Wakefield, the residence of Mr Rowland Winn, MP. The weather was fine, and the attendance was variously estimated at from thirty to sixty thousand, the grounds of the Priory being thrown open to the public from a very early hour in the morning, and several towns of the Riding sending large contingents.

This was one of several Conservative rallies hosted by Rowland Winn at his Yorkshire seat at Nostell Priory. He was made a Lord of the Treasury, and thus a junior Whip, during Benjamin Disraeli's administration, Chief Whip in 1880 and, following further party gatherings at Nostell, he was awarded a peerage when the Conservatives returned to government following the 1885 general election, despite not winning the most seats, or the popular vote.

Leeds Mercury, **Saturday, 30 September 1876**
ROBBERY AT NOSTELL DURING THE CONSERVATIVE DEMONSTRATION
On Wednesday evening, during the great demonstration of Conservatives at Nostell Priory, the occasion seems to have been favourable to some thief or thieves in robbing the house known as the [Spread] Eagle Inn, at Wragby, and near to the Priory. The house is kept by Robert Whitaker, and it appears that during the demonstration the house was thronged with visitors. Advantage was taken of the occasion to carry away the sum of £52 in notes and gold. The property carried away is

one £10 cheque drawn on Cox and Co., Craig's-court Charing-cross, and endorsed 'John Shelton'; three £5 notes, one of which is a Bank of England (No. 94,329) and nearly new; and £27 in sovereigns and half sovereigns. The police in the district are making every inquiry into the circumstances of the robbery, and it is to be hoped the perpetrators will be found out. Several attempts were made at picking pockets on the occasion of the demonstration, and one or two apprehensions were made by the police.

Leeds Times, Saturday, 7 October 1876
ATTEMPTING TO PICK A DETECTIVE'S POCKET

At the Pontefract Court House, on Saturday, James Haley, of Bradford, was charged with attempting to pick the pocket of Police-officer Willmore, at Nostell Station, on the night of the 27th September. Detective Gregg stated that on the day of the Conservative demonstration at Nostell Priory he and two other officers in plain clothes were awaiting the arrival of the train for Wakefield at Nostell Station in the evening. The crush was very great on the platform, and the witness felt a person's hand moving under his elbow, and, suspecting the cause, he raised his arm still higher, when suddenly seizing the wrist of the hand he felt, he found the prisoner's hand was in Police-officer Willmore's pocket. Prisoner, who is an old offender, having been previously convicted for pilfering, was now sentenced by the Bench to one month's imprisonment with hard labour.

Sheffield Daily Telegraph, Thursday, 2 November 1876
DESTRUCTIVE FIRE NEAR PONTEFRACT
SUPPOSED INCENDIARISM
SPECIAL TELEGRAPH

Pontefract, Wednesday night. This morning the stackyard of Messrs W. and H. Scholey, Huntwick Farm, on the estate of Mr Rowland Winn, MP, Nostell Priory, near Pontefract, was discovered to be on fire, and resulted in the total destruction of seventeen stacks of wheat, and the product of 400 acres. The damage is estimated at nearly £3,000. The fire-engines from Nostell Priory and Pontefract arrived just in time to save the farmstead.

Nostell Station, shown during a strike in 1912.

The origin of the fire is a mystery, but supposed to be the work of an incendiary. The fire is still burning.

Sheffield Independent, Saturday, 28 January 1882

Mr and Mrs Rowland Winn have had a full house at Nostell for the Wakefield ball, and have done their duty to their neighbours by themselves giving a capital dance at the Priory.

Sheffield Independent, Thursday, 16 November 1882
THE NOSTELL POACHING AFFRAY

Yesterday, at Pontefract, Timothy Derbyshire, of Purston, and Samuel Slater, of South Featherstone, both miners, were charged with being concerned in the night poaching affray at Nostell Priory, near Pontefract, on the 9th inst. James Purdon, keeper on the Nostell estate, said on the morning of the 9th, about 2.30, he and several other keepers were secreted in the top park at Nostell Priory, near the Obelisk Lodge, when about sixteen poachers entered the park. Several began to fix netting. The keepers rushed out, and the poachers ran off after throwing a volley of stones. They left on the field four nets, one 277 yards, five bags, ten rabbits, bludgeons, stones, pegs, and a black felt hat. On visiting the houses of the prisoners the same morning about 5 a.m. they were not at home. Police-sergeant Millar, stationed at Purston, identified the hat found in the park as that worn by Derbyshire. The prisoner Slater had been convicted nine times, and was engaged in the serious affray on the same estate when the keeper, Joseph Bull, was nearly murdered. The bench sentenced Slater to six months' imprisonment with hard labour, and ordered him to find sureties, himself in £20 and two in £10 each, for twelve months, or to undergo a further term of three months; Derbyshire was sentenced to two months' hard labour. Other warrants have been issued.

The previous affray occurred in August 1879, when Joseph Bull became entangled in one of the poachers' nets. They proceeded to beat him senseless with their bludgeons. Arrests were made and some of the perpetrators were sent to prison.

Yorkshire Post and Leeds Intelligencer, **Wednesday, 24 January 1883**
MARRIAGE OF LORD CLONCURRY AND MISS WINN AT NOSTELL PRIORY

Valentine Frederick Lawless, Lord Cloncurry, of Lyons Castle, Kildare and Miss Laura Sophia Priscilla Winn, the eldest daughter of Mr Rowland Winn, one of the members for North Lincolnshire, were married yesterday at Nostell Priory. The event was regarded with much interest in the wide circle of relatives and friends of the two families immediately concerned, the surrounding gentry, and the tenantry of Mr Winn's Nostell and Appleby estates; and it is a long time since Nostell Priory itself, excepting on politically significant occasions, was the scene of so much merry-making as it was yesterday. The old baronial residence which, thanks to the open-handed hospitality of its esteemed host, Yorkshire people know so well, has been gradually filling with guests during the last fortnight, each train stopping at the little wayside station bringing a party of distinguished personage, from town or from their country seats north and south. Nearly everybody who had accepted an invitation to the wedding had arrived at the Priory on Monday, Mr Winn's dinner party on Monday evening including forty or fifty members of various county families. A special train from Appleby yesterday morning conveyed to Nostell nearly 200 of the occupiers of the North Lincolnshire estates of Mr Winn. The numerous tenants of the family in and around Nostell rode, drove, or walked thither; and many visitors from Pontefract, Wakefield, Doncaster, and the intervening places arrived early enough to stroll through the ample demesne before they and the villagers crowded the trim little church, which stands just within the Priory grounds, and in which the members of the Winn family and the present and former occupants of the long rows of snug looking dwellings which constitutes the village have worshipped for many generations. Many of those who wished to see the wedding, and who, having by means of tickets, of which a limited number had been distributed by the Priory steward, succeeded in passing the policemen at the park gates, were a little uncertain as to the exact hour fixed for the event; so they lingered in groups beside the flight of steps in the centre of the spacious façade of the mansion, or took up favourable positions likely to afford a peep at the bridal party on their way to or from church. Shortly after eleven a carriage and pair drove down the short stretch of coach-road from the Priory to the church with an instalment of guests, and within a quarter of an hour or so the side aisles or lady chapel of the sanctuary, including the family pews of the Winns, were filled by a bright and happy looking assemblage of expectant ladies and gentlemen.

The bride wore a white brocaded velvet dress, trimmed with Brussels lace, a tulle veil, and wreath of orange blossom fastened by five diamond stars, the gift of Lord Cloncurry. Miss Winn's other adornments included a diamond pendant given by her father; and three bracelets, one set with pearls and diamonds a present from the Lady Dowager Cloncurry; another similarly ornamented, an offering from the Appleby tenantry; the third being the gift of Mr James Winn, one of her brothers.

The bride and bridegroom lunched hastily apart from the company, for they had arranged to travel to London by express out of Leeds, which was to stop specially for them at Nostell.

After the couple had gone the remainder of the day at the Priory was given up to merry-making in which all comers were free to join.

The interior of the church at Wragby.

York Herald, **Saturday, 22 March 1884**
SUPPOSED SUICIDE

On Thursday the dead body of Maria Webb, aged 19 years, a domestic servant with the Rev. Mr Hughes, curate of Wragby, was found in the Upper Lake at Nostell Priory. The young woman was missed from her situation on Saturday morning, and was met near to where she was found by a groom at Nostell Priory. She was noticed to be in low spirits for some time past, and it is supposed she committed suicide.

Yorkshire Gazette, **Saturday, 30 August 1884**
GREAT CONSERVATIVE GATHERING AT NOSTELL PRIORY

One of the largest gathering of Conservatives ever seen in England was held on Saturday at Nostell Priory, the residence of Mr Rowland Winn. It is estimated that upwards of 120,000 people were present. More than 200 Conservative Associations were represented at this demonstration. At 12.25 the deputations from Associations, Clubs, and Registration Committees met near the Riding School, and shortly afterwards Sir Stafford Northcote and Lord Carnarvon received about two hundred addresses. Most of them were addressed to the Leader of the Opposition.

Sir Stafford Northcote briefly addressed them. He said it was no small labour to acknowledge so many even in the most summary way. That morning's experience, the reception of nearly 200 addresses, however, was unique. There was one thing which they had to regret very much – the absence of Lord Randolph Churchill, who at the last moment had found himself unable to attend. The meeting about to be held would be greatly noticed in the country, not only for its size, but also for its representative character. It would show that the people who attended were not idlers who came to spend a pleasant summer's day in ducal park; but men who were regularly and daily working to support the Conservative cause.

Shields Daily Gazette, **Thursday, 4 September 1884**
THE NUMBERS AT NOSTELL PRIORY

The *Leeds Mercury* has pursued its investigations into the numbers of demonstrators attending the Tory demonstration at Nostell Priory and now reports as follows: When the meeting took place, Mr Rowland Winn announced that a careful computation had been made of the numbers, and that it had been ascertained that *more than one hundred and twenty thousand persons* were present. Anxious to do justice to the promotors of the meeting, we have taken pains to ascertain, in the most accurate manner, the actual number of persons conveyed by railway to Nostell and Sharlston stations on the day of the demonstration. We find that this number falls short of *twenty-five thousand*. Nostell is five miles from the nearest town, Pontefract, and the day of the meeting was one of the hottest of the summer. It may be assumed therefore that not many persons walked to the Park. A considerable number were, however, conveyed from Barnsley, Pontefract, and Wakefield in waggonettes. Making the amplest allowance for those who travelled to the scene of meeting in this manner, as well as for those who walked, we are brought to the conclusion that the actual attendance at the demonstration, instead of being 120,000 as stated by Mr Rowland Winn, or 50,000 as stated by us, was little more than 30,000. We place this calculation with the greatest confidence before our readers, as being one which approximates most closely to the truth; and we leave the promoters of the demonstration to impugn our estimate if they can.

Stamford Mercury, Friday, 5 December 1884

APPLEBY – Nov. 19, at the Hall, Priscilla widow of Charles Winn, Esq., of Nostell Priory, Yorks. And youngest daughter of the late Sir Wm. Srickland, Bart., of Boynton, 88.

York Herald, Saturday, 6 December 1884

By the death of Mrs Winn, mother of Mr Rowland Winn, MP, a venerable figure is removed from the best social and political circles of South Yorkshire and the Lincolnshire seat of the family, and her house was the centre and focus of all the Conservative activity in the district. She had attained her eighty-eighth year.

Yorkshire Evening Press, Thursday, 9 April 1885

Thomas Moore, *alias*, William McCarthy, 62, fish hawker, and who has spent a great portion of his life in prison, was sentenced to five years' penal servitude and three years' police supervision for stealing fowls, at Nostell.

The Conservative Demonstration held at Nostell Priory on 30 August 1884, as depicted in *The Illustrated Sporting and Dramatic News*.

Yorkshire Post and Leeds Intelligencer, **Friday, 26 June 1885**
A PEERAGE FOR MR ROWLAND WINN

The Queen has been pleased to confer a peerage on Mr Rowland Winn, MP, under the style of Baron St Oswald of Nostell, in the county of York. Mr Winn's seat was vacated yesterday afternoon by his acceptance of the Chiltern Hundreds. Mr Akers-Douglas, MP, will become Whip to the Conservative party and Patronage Secretary to the Treasury.

Mr Winn is the son of the late Mr Charles Winn, of Nostell Priory, Yorkshire, and of Appleby Hall, Lincolnshire, his mother being a daughter of the late Sir William Strickland, Bart. He was born in 1820, and married in 1854 the daughter of the late Colonel Damaresq, and niece of the fifth Earl of Lanesborough. Mr Winn was educated at Trinity College, Cambridge. He entered Parliament in 1868, being returned without opposition as one of the members for North Lincolnshire; and at the dissolution in 1874 he was again returned without opposition. Being appointed a Secretary to the Treasury in the Conservative Ministry that then acceded to power, his seat became vacant, and he was re-elected without opposition. In 1880 he was once again returned, so that he has sat continuously for North Lincolnshire for a period of 17 years. Mr Winn during his whole Parliamentary career has been a consistent and energetic supporter of Conservatism, and has not confined his efforts to the division of Lincolnshire which he represented in the House of Commons, but has with equal ardour given his influence to the cause in West Yorkshire. For many years he was the chairman of the Conservative Association in the Southern Division of the West Riding, and the great political demonstrations which from time to time during the last ten years have been held at his beautiful seat at Nostell are now matters of history. One of these great demonstrations was in 1876, when the speakers included Sir Stafford Northcote (now Earl of Iddesleigh) and Lord George Hamilton. The last demonstration was held a year ago, and was in support of the action of the House of Lords in regard to the Franchise Bill, and was one of the most significant as it was one of the largest gatherings held during that agitation. Addresses expressing confidence in the leaders of the Opposition to the number of nearly 200 were presented to Sir Stafford Northcote (who was the principal speaker) by as many Conservative associations in the country. The speakers also included Earl Carnarvon. Mr Winn has officiated as one of the Conservative whips for a number of years.

MR BELTON, THE STEWARD

Thomas Belton, steward at Nostell Priory.

Leeds Mercury, **Monday, 8 February 1886**

SUDDEN DEATH OF BARON ST OSWALD'S AGENT

On Saturday night Mr Thomas Belton, of Nostell, who had for upwards of half a century acted as agent for Baron St Oswald, and his father, expired suddenly at this residence at Nostell. The deceased gentleman, who was a widower and about 82 years of age, had not been in very good health for some time past; but he visited Wakefield on Friday in company with a grandson who resided with him, and transacted business at several places. Early on Saturday morning he became seriously indisposed, and remained in an unconscious state all the day. He expired shortly before seven o'clock the same evening. The deceased gentleman was well known and very highly respected by his employer, the tenants on the estate and others.

Leeds Mercury, **Wednesday, 16 February 1887**

ATTEMPT TO DEFRAUD LORD ST OSWALD

At the Town Hall, Pontefract, on Monday, John William Wilson, a brush maker, of Bradford, was charged with attempting to obtain money by false pretences and begging letters from Lord St Oswald, of Nostell Priory, on the 3rd instant. Lord St Oswald gave evidence showing that he received a letter on the 3rd instant to the effect that a committee had been formed in the town to alleviate distress existing, that it had been decided to give a treat to 500 persons, and soliciting subscriptions to the fund. The letter was signed 'J.W. Wilson, chairman'. The letter was sent by Lord St Oswald to

Mr D. Longstaff, of Pontefract, chairman of the Conservative Association, for inquiries to be made. Mr D. Longstaff said he received the letter in question, and handed it to Mr Fearnside, Chief Constable, and also caused to be forwarded a post-office order addressed to the party named in the letter, at the York Post-office, till called for. Inquiries were made, and the letter found to be false in every particular, and the writer was arrested when calling at the post-office for the letter addressed to him. He said that since he failed in business, ten years ago, he had been much reduced, and his life had been one of painful endurance and hardship.

York Herald, Saturday, 26 January 1889
SUICIDE NEAR PONTEFRACT

On Saturday, an inquest was held at No 50, Nostell-row, Nostell, near Pontefract, touching the death of Joseph Atack, banksman, employed at Nostell Colliery, owned by Lord St Oswald. The deceased, who was a married man, and leaves a wife and four children, had fancied in his own mind that a recent accident at the colliery was attributable to his conduct, and that he would be committed for manslaughter. This was a delusion on his part. On Friday morning he was missed, and was subsequently found drowned in Nostell Dam, in about four feet of water. A verdict of 'Temporary insanity' was returned.

Dundee Evening Telegraph, Monday, 6 January 1890
EARTHENWARE PIPES FOR ELECTRIC WIRES

Earthenware pipes are now strongly recommended for the conveyance of electric wires underground. A splendid installation has been effected in this way by Lord St Oswald at Nostell Priory.

St James's Gazette, Saturday, 12 April 1890
SERIOUS ILLNESS OF LORD ST OSWALD

Lord St Oswald was suddenly attacked with apoplexy after returning home to Nostell Priory, near Wakefield, on Thursday evening, from a meeting at which he appeared to be in good health and spirits. Three medical gentlemen were summoned from Leeds, Wakefield, and Ackworth, and Lady St Oswald reached the Priory from their town residence shortly after midnight. The noble lord remained unconscious until yesterday afternoon, and last evening he was progressing as favourably as could be expected.

York Herald, Thursday, 5 February 1891
MURDEROUS ASSUALT ON A GAMEKEEPER

At the West Riding Court, Pontefract, yesterday, before Mr W.F. Tempest and Dr Kemp, John Taylor, miner, of Hemsworth, was charged, in custody, with assaulting Henry Eddy, under gamekeeper to Lord St Oswald, on the Nostell estate, on the 26th January last. Mr Kaberry prosecuted. On the 26th January prisoner and another man (not in custody) were on the Nostell estate poaching, and were accosted by the keeper, who saw them with a ferret, and a net over a rabbit hole. The keeper asked them what they were doing there, and without any reason the prisoner knocked the keeper down and called for his mate 'Boxer', and both set to work in kicking him on the head. The keeper was very seriously injured, being badly cut on the head and face. He was rendered almost helpless, but attempted to follow them, when the two poachers turned round and threatened to 'do for him' if he followed them further, and was about to throw him into a beck. Dr Wood, of Ackworth, gave evidence as to the dangerous condition of the keeper after the assault, and was surprised at his rapid recovery. The prisoner, it was shown, had been many times convicted previously, even for assaulting his own mother. The Bench remarked that it was a most unprovoked and murderous assault. An example must be made to put down kicking, and prisoner would be sent to prison for three months with hard labour, and if the costs, £1 15s were not paid, a further one month's imprisonment.

Diss Express, Friday, 14 October 1892
A GUARDSMAN'S WEDDING

At the fashionable London church of St George's, Hanover-square, the marriage took place on Monday of the Honourable Rowland Winn, MP for Pontefract, of the Coldstream Guards, and eldest son of Lord and Lady St Oswald, of Nostell Priory, near Wakefield, and of Appleby Hall, Lincolnshire, with Miss Mabel Forbes, the youngest daughter of the late Sir Charles Forbes, Bart., of Newe, Aberdeenshire, and Helen Lady Forbes, and a niece of Georgina Countess of Dudley, and also of the Duchess of Athole. The wedding ceremony was fully choral, and was performed by the Rev Canon Cross, late Rector of Appleby, Lincolnshire, assisted by the Rev David Anderson, the Rector of St George's. The soldiers of the bridegroom's company of the Coldstream Guards lined the aisle. The church was prettily decorated with palms and white flowers. The bride was accompanied by her brother, Sir Charles Stewart Forbes, of Newe who led her up the aisle. The bridegroom had, as best man, the Marquis of Winchester, a brother officer in the Coldstream Guards.

During the afternoon the Hon Rowland and Mrs Winn left for Welbeck Abbey, which has been lent for the honeymoon by the Duke of Portland. The presents were exceptionally beautiful and of great value. The Prince

Mabel Forbes in later life as Lady St Oswald.

and Princess of Wales gave a diamond, pearl and sapphire dagger; Princesses Victoria, and Maud of Wales, a gold and diamond horseshoe brooch; the borough of Pontefract (the bridegroom's constituency), a complete silver dessert service; and the officers of the Coldstream Guards, two silver candelabra and a silver bowl.

Yorkshire Evening Post, Friday, 20 January 1893

Lord St Oswald died last night at Nostell Priory. For many days he has been wrestling with sickness, and it was hoped that his sound constitution and reserve strength would pull him through. But at the age of seventy-three a serious illness too often proves fatal. Lord St Oswald was better known as Mr Rowland Winn, the hard-working whip of the Conservative party, whose vigilance and coolness came into play in the memorable divisions. His work, the patient, untiring work of keeping the party together, was not so well known; but its importance was ever felt. The title will go to the eldest son, the Hon Rowland Winn, who has sat for Pontefract since the 1885 election.

Morning Post, Saturday, 1 July 1893

The will of the late Lord St Oswald, of Nostell Priory, near Wakefield, who died on the 19th of January last, has been proved by the acting executor, his son Rowland, now second Baron St Oswald, power being reserved to grant probate to Baroness St Oswald, the relict. To her the testator bequeathed £1,000 and (in addition to her jointure under settlements) a jointure of £900 a year during the lifetime of his mother, to be increased on her death to £1,400 a year. He bequeathed to each of his younger children £10,000, and to his daughters Emily Louisa and Maud Julia whilst unmarried, after the death of their mother, annuities of £400 each, or if one only should remain unmarried an annuity to her of £600. Lord St Oswald devised all his real estate to the present Lord St Oswald, and bequeathed the residue of his personal estate to the person who, having attained the age of 21 years, should after his death, first become entitled to his real estate. The gross value of the personal estate has been valued at £84,311, and the net value at nil.

Yorkshire Evening Post, **Saturday, 14 October 1893**
INTIMIDATING WORKMEN AT NOSTELL
CHARGED BY MOUNTED POLICE

In the vicinity of Nostell Colliery there have been signs of trouble during the past few days, and yesterday one of the by-workmen was reported to have been injured by the locked-out colliers for having been at work.

News having reached Pontefract of the expressed intention of the men to prevent the by-workers going to the colliery this morning, six mounted police (Superintendent Whincup and Inspector Cooper and four men of the London Mounted Constabulary) left Pontefract this morning at 3.30 for Nostell.

They reached the entrance to Nostell Priory, the seat of Lord St Oswald, between four and five o'clock, and here found some fifty men congregated, with small lights, evidently awaiting to carry out the threats to prevent workmen going to the colliery.

The order was given for the mounted police to charge, and this they did right smartly, several of the colliers receiving strokes from the flat side of the policemen's swords, whilst one man was trampled under the feet of one of the horses, and is reported to be lamed. The colliers flew in every direction, but the mounted police were drawn away by the blowing of the colliery buzzer, and fearing that something was wrong there they galloped off at full speed to the colliery. They found all safe there, however, the pit premises being guarded by ten of the local police and seven of the Metropolitan Police.

The miners all cleared away, and, therefore, the mounted police were withdrawn, and arrived back at Pontefract this forenoon at 9.30.

London Evening Standard, **Tuesday, 25 December 1894**

At Featherstone, near Pontefract, on Friday night, three men, named George Henry Collett, Fred Micklethwaite, and William Cawley, were returning home at twenty minutes past eleven, when they found Francis Larcombe, head gamekeeper to Lord St Oswald, of Nostell Priory, lying in an almost helpless state of drunkenness opposite the Featherstone Local Board offices. Collett lifted Larcombe to his feet, and with the assistance of his companions was leading him along the road when they met a young man named Henry King, a miner of Wakefield. On seeing King, Larcombe stopped and said,

'I will give you fellows a drink,' and pulling a revolver from a breast pocket he deliberately fired at King. The ball penetrated the unfortunate man's breast, and he died almost immediately. Larcombe, who is a married man with a family, was taken into custody and formally charged before and remanded by the West Riding Magistrates at Pontefract until Thursday next.

Yorkshire Evening Post, Saturday, 16 March 1895
FOUR MONTHS FOR LARCOMBE

Mr Justice Kennedy in the Crown Court at the Leeds Assizes to–day, passed sentence upon Francis Larcombe (40), late gamekeeper to Lord St Oswald, of Nostell Priory, who had been found guilty of the manslaughter of Henry King, at Purston Jaglin, on December 21. The prisoner, on being asked if he had anything to say, said that on the night in question he went to Pontefract on business, and not on pleasure. He had only four small whiskies during the day. He had no idea how that amount of whisky could have affected him so much. Whether it was the whisky, or whether he was drugged, he did not know. He had his suspicions. He appealed to his lordship to take into consideration that he had lost his situation and character, and that he had a wife and family. He had also lost the benefits of a society to which he had subscribed for nearly 20 years. The Judge said that, looking at the prisoner's past character, and the facts which came out at the trial, it was a case with which he was able to deal without passing any severe sentence. He hoped what had happened would be a lesson to the prisoner and others to refrain from carrying about the roads loaded revolvers, and would also be a warning to the prisoner to abstain from liquors. He was sentenced to four months' imprisonment.

Lincolnshire Free Press, Tuesday, 1 February 1898

Major Winn, of the Rifle Brigade, has been killed by a fall from his pony playing polo at Umballa, in India. Much regret will be felt in North Lincolnshire at the news. Major Winn was brother to Lord St Oswald, being the second son of the late Lord St Oswald, of Nostell Priory, who for so many years was MP for North Lincolnshire. He was born in 1858, joined the Rifle Brigade in 1879, was promoted to a captaincy in 1888, and obtained the rank of major in 1896. He has acted as aide-de-camp to the General commanding at Gibraltar.

The memorial in the church at Wragby to Major Charles Winn.

Chapter 6

The Third Lord St Oswald

Anything but the average chorus girl.

On 29 July 1914, Eton-educated Rowland George Winn, the eldest son of the second Lord St Oswald and his wife Lady Mabel, turned twenty-one and lavish celebrations to honour his coming of age were held at Nostell over several days. Less than a week later, Germany, who had invaded Belgium on 24 July, ignored a British ultimatum to get out by 3 August. The following day, the British declared war. By early November, provincial newspapers were reporting that young Rowland Winn, who was a second lieutenant in the Coldstream Guards and had left for France as soon as war broke out, had been wounded in action, the War Office having initially informed his distraught parents that he had been killed. Twelve months later, Rowland made headlines across the world.

His name had appeared in the papers as early as 1912, when, a year after finishing his education at Eton, he was training as a cadet at Sandhurst Military Academy. He'd been admitted to Sandhurst on 31 January 1912, performing reasonably well in his exams – he was especially competent at history, riding, musketry and physical training, though by no means top of the class.

On 10 October 1912, the *Yorkshire Evening Post* reported that the cadet had been in trouble with the police:

At Camberley today, the Hon Rowland George Winn, a Sandhurst cadet was fined £10 for dangerously driving a motor car.

Defendant drove the car at what witness described as a terrific speed into a cab which was knocked over, and its occupants flung out.

Rowland kept his name out the press for the rest of the year and graduated from Sandhurst in December 1913, joining the Coldstream Guards the following January. Then in April 1914, the *Reading Mercury* reported that he had been the victim of an attempted deception. In February, a valet named James Fraser, aged thirty-three, had called at Victoria Barracks, where Rowland was based, and attempted to obtain the sum of fifteen shillings from him. The police were called and Fraser was convicted and sentenced to six weeks in prison, the recorder preferring a lenient punishment to afford the valet another chance.

July saw the start of the coming of age celebrations at Nostell. On the young man's birthday the famous old site held a luncheon in a marquee that had been erected in the grounds. Five hundred guests representing the Lincolnshire Iron Masters' Association, tradespeople from Wakefield and Pontefract, the Yorkshire tenants, estate employees, and the officials of the Nostell Colliery gathered to enjoy the first day's festivities, and replying to a toast in his family's honour, Rowland's father, Lord St Oswald, said:

> I hope that as long as we live you will always find us ready to help, and to do all we can for those who are suffering or in distress. I can assure you that it will be our duty to assist those who are in any way down on their luck, down at heels, and down because of illness.

The following day the colliers themselves, along with their wives and children, were the special guests at Nostell, and around 1,300 were treated to a tea, a selection of music from the local Featherstone Brass Band, and were given as a gift a pipe and an ounce of tobacco, which, the *Leeds Mercury* informed its readers, 'they "reeked" to their hearts' content.'

Word of the festivities even appeared in *The Tatler* magazine. 'Very high jinks of Nostell', its early August edition declared. The reporter described a 'regular party of young people – Lady Irene Curzon and Count Michael Torby, and Violet de Trafford and Phyllis Combe, and a crowd of young men'. Apparently parties at Nostell were fewer nowadays as 'Lady St Oswald's health can't stand the strain of much entertaining, and she, too, only comes in summer to the lovely old house, full of Chippendale furniture – and gorgeous pictures and goodness knows what else in the way of household gods and treasures.'

Saturday, 1 August 1914 was also the date of Lord St Oswald's fifty-eighth birthday and celebrations were duly extended to mark that occasion as well.

'Long Row', Nostell, where colliers employed at the Winn family colliery resided.

A toast he gave during the merrymaking was recorded in the *Sheffield Daily Telegraph*, which stated that when he addressed the guests, he adopted a sombre, foreboding tone:

> his Lordship alluded to the catastrophe which threatened to overwhelm Europe. Whether England would be dragged into this conflict or not no man could say. He was glad to say that in the face of this great danger Party politics had been dropped, and all sides were united with the object of securing peace. At the same time, there was no saying how soon a match might light the squib, and the inevitable explosion would follow, which would be a sad thing for this country and for all the countries in Europe.

On 5 November, the *Yorkshire Post and Leeds Intelligencer* wrote not of luncheons and toasts but of the dead and wounded of the war in Europe, one of whom was 'Sec. Lieut. the Hon Rowland Winn (wounded)'. His injuries, sustained in France, were at first mistakenly thought to be fatal, but he rallied and came back to Nostell, where he recuperated, spending Christmas 1914 with his family. By this time Nostell Priory had been requisitioned and the *Leeds Mercury* reported that it had 'been placed at disposal of the St John Ambulance Association' to be used as a convalescent home. Clearly, Rowland's recovery, from what the *Leeds Mercury* described in December as a 'serious injury', was quick because the *Yorkshire Post and Leeds Intelligencer* reported that he'd been promoted to a full lieutenancy. On 21 April 1915, *The Tatler* published a photograph of the officers of the 2nd Battalion, Coldstream Guards, with Rowland Winn standing in the back row.

If Rowland was a subscriber to *Tatler* magazine and had thumbed through an edition published in March of the previous year, he might have noticed the photograph of a beautiful young actress called Evie Carew, who was appearing at Daly's theatre, off Leicester Square, in a production of the musical comedy *The Marriage Market*. *Tatler* reader or not, Miss Carew would soon catch the young heir's eye.

Evie had joined Daly's as a chorus girl in 1911 when the theatre was staging *The Count of Luxembourg*, which opened in May of that year. At that time, Evie was known by her birth name, Nellie Greene, and she was living in a flat in Bathurst Mansions on Holloway Road in London. This was the

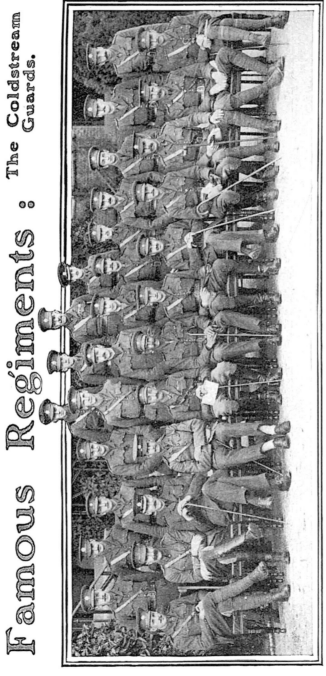

Famous Regiments : The Coldstream Guards.

Russell & Sons, Windsor

THE OFFICERS OF THE 2ND BATTALION, COLDSTREAM GUARDS

From left to right are : Top row—2nd Lieut. C. J. Darwin, Hon. R. G. Winn, Hon. Captain Wright, 2nd Lieut. W. G. Shaw-Stewart; second row—Lieut. C. L. Gordon, 2nd Lieut. A. H. M. Ramsay, Lieut. H. W. Verelst, 2nd Lieut. Lord Marsham, Lieut. H. C. Loyd, Lieut. R. G. Graves-Sawle, Lieut. R. L. Bewicke-Copley, 2nd Lieut. R. W. Lockwood, Lieut. Lord Petre, Lieut. L. M. Gibbs, 2nd Lieut. E. de Trafford, Lieut. H. Legge-Bourke, Captain " Byng," Hopwood; third row—Lieut. A. Leigh-Bennett, Captain Sinclair, R.A.M.C., Captain J. H. Phillips, Major P. A. Macgregor, D.S.O., Major R. A. Markham, Lieut.-Colonel C. E. Pereira, D.S.O., Lieut. and Adjutant A. C. Dawnay, Captain F. Hardy, Captain H. M. Pryce Jones, Captain G. B. S. Follet, Captain J. Egerton, Captain Sir W. B. Barttelot, Bart.

Rowland Winn with his fellow guardsmen.

home of her sister, Albina Maud Ward, and her brother-in-law, John Percival Ward, who'd married Albina in 1906.

Nellie had been born in early May 1890 in Bradford in the West Riding of Yorkshire (just a few miles from Nostell Priory) to Charles and Albina Greene. The family soon moved to Canton in Glamorganshire, where Charles worked as a nailer. However, the lure of London was too much to resist and the family moved to the capital. In May 1899, Nellie began attending Prospect Terrace School in St Pancras, which had opened a few years earlier, and in 1901 the census records the family at Cadogan Gardens, near Sloane Square. By now Charles was working as a caretaker and his son and namesake, seventeen-year-old Charles Greene, was described as being 'employed on [the] stage'. The census taken in 1911 revealed that the older Charles had become a restaurant manager, he and his wife Albina living at Devonshire Road in Holloway.

A year later, Daly's, under the management of musical theatre giant George Edwardes, was staging *Gipsy Love*, an operetta about a romance between people from opposing classes. This was followed by *The Marriage Market*, which opened in May 1913 to pretty good reviews.

In April 1915, Edwardes brought a production called *Betty* to London; it had been playing at the Prince's Theatre in Manchester since December 1914. The plot of this musical comedy was centred on Gerard, a young member of the nobility whose father, the Duke of Crowborough, was becoming tired with his son's wayward lifestyle. Frustrated with his father's constant badgering, and after being humiliated by the older man in front of his friends, Gerard decided to marry a kitchen maid called Betty, the character who gave the play its name. He hoped this would upset his father. But instead of turning on his daughter-in-law, the duke provided Betty with Gerard's allowance, and through her charming manner she was able to convince the upper-class society into which she had entered to accept her, and she and her husband lived happily ever after. Anything but the average kitchen maid, it would seem.

Evie appeared in the chorus of this production, which ran for 391 performances, and in April 1915, the month the show opened in London, she featured with the rest of the chorus in *Tatler*, forming a 'bevy of beauty'.

Reviews were positive, a critic describing it as 'worthy of Mr George Edwardes' best productions', and another calling it 'a feast of fashions'

MERMAIDS FROM "THE MARRIAGE MARKET"

Darlings from Daly's Doing a Dip.

"SHOOTING THE SHUTE"—FAIR SWIMMERS FROM DALY'S THEATRE

Where Mr. George Edwardes's great success, "The Marriage Market," is still going strong. The order of starting for the great diving act depicted above is: Miss Veda le Grand, Miss Evie Carew, Miss Jean Stirling, Miss Kate Zoller, Miss Evelyn Drew, Miss Elsie Spencer, and Miss Irene Flower

Evie Carew shown in March 1914, with her fellow performers in a publicity shot for *The Marriage Market.*

" BETTY " BEAUTIES

Who will Appear in the Postponed Production at Daly's.

MISS DOROTHY FUNSTON   MISS IRENE FLOWER   MISS MADELINE SEYMOUR

MISS DAISY LINNELL   MISS STELLA RIGA   MISS EVIE CAREW

MISS GLADYS SQUIRE   MISS DOROTHY STANMORE   MISS BERYL NORMAN

After a successful début at Manchester "Betty" has arrived in town, and the first London production will be given at Daly's Theatre at an early date. This musical comedy—in which as usual a bevy of beauty will be seen, including the charming ladies pictured above—is the work of Miss Gladys Unger and Mr. Frederick Lonsdale, with lyrics by Mr. Adrian Ross and music by Mr. Paul Rubens. All the above studies are by Mr. E. O. Hoppé.

Evie in April 1915, with the other girls appearing in *Betty* at Daly's theatre.

and 'one of the most charming [shows] of its kind'. 'Cinderella in modern society' was how one reviewer summed up the plot.

Perhaps Rowland spent a few hours in the audience having heard about this fashionable new production. If so, was his gaze fixed on the Yorkshire-born nailer's daughter in the chorus? Did the story he was watching stir something in the young man whose life had almost been extinguished just months earlier?

Eight months later, on 27 December 1915, an explosive exclusive appeared on the second page of that morning's *Daily Mirror*. 'PEER'S HEIR WEDS A CHORUS GIRL' screamed the headline. 'BEAUTIFUL BRIDE WHO FORMERLY PLAYED IN *BETTY*' claimed the subheading.

If they subscribed to the newspaper it was enough to make Lord and Lady St Oswald choke on their cornflakes. The report explained that the Hon. Rowland Winn, 'heir of a well-known peer of the realm', had secretly married 'one of the most beautiful and charming chorus girls on the London stage'. The couple, and a small number of close friends, had managed to keep the marriage out of the press for eight weeks, the sensational wedding having taken place at St Saviour's Church in Paddington on 29 October. A special licence had been granted, presumably to avoid the necessity of the public reading of banns, and the reporter reckoned that 'the number of people who knew of it as late as yesterday could be counted on the fingers of one hand.' The reporter was certain that not one of Rowland's 'nearest relatives have been aware of the romance, and will probably learn of it for the first time this morning.'

On the day of the wedding, the vicar of St Saviour's had waited patiently for the couple to arrive, but when twenty-five minutes after the appointed time had ticked by, he presumed the ceremony had been called off and left the church. Rowland was running late, having to travel to London from Windsor, where his regiment was based (though his home address was 17 Hill Street, Berkeley Square at this time). And then it transpired that the best man, Captain Wentworth of the Royal Flying Corps, who was due to fly to London that morning, had been detained at his base and had abandoned plans to attend.

Undeterred, the excited couple strode up to the church, where they were met by the vestry clerk, who told them that nobody was on hand to marry them. Undaunted, Rowland handed the keys to his motorcar to the clerk, who hurried around the capital looking for somebody to perform the ceremony. Luckily he found St Saviour's junior curate, Reverend Geoffrey S. Clarke, who was ushered to the church to marry the pair. The marriage was witnessed by Alfred Douse, the verger, and William Healey Matthew, the very clerk who found the curate. It was these two men alone who signed the marriage entry as witnesses, an entry that appears in the parish registers for St Saviour's Church, Paddington. Despite not knowing a thing about the marriage, the baronet's name and occupation were recorded on the entry, these details having been supplied by the groom when asked for particulars about his father. They read: 'Rowland Baron St Oswald, Peer of the Realm.' But it would be several months before Lord and Lady St Oswald would meet Evie.

The *Daily Mirror* reporter went on to describe the bride, who married under her real name, Nellie Greene, as 'uncommonly beautiful', adding that news of her wedding would come as a 'great surprise' to her friends, who, they wrote, describe her as a 'very charming girl, with the most lovable disposition'.

The story, which featured photographs of the couple, reproduced in *Tatler* the following month, was picked up by the provincial press, the national press and even the international press, the *New York Times* printing the story later that day, though they got their noble titles mixed up, promoting Lord St Oswald to the rank of earl!

On 3 April the following year, Rowland wrote a letter to his father on Coldstream Guards' letter-headed paper in which he referred to his parents' first ever meeting with his wife, which had only just taken place. Whether his father was as 'impressed' by Evie as Rowland wrote, cannot be determined from the contents of this letter alone, but he was certainly keen to extol his new bride's virtues.

My Dear Pa,

Just a line to say how very pleased I was to hear from mummy that you had met my wife.

As far as I could gather from mummy's letter you were favourably impressed & liked her. At any rate she wrote & told me you were extremely nice to her; & I only hope [you] really understand that she is anything but the average 'chorus-girl'.

THE HON. ROWLAND WINN *Lafayette*

Who is also in the Coldstream Guards, and is Lord and Lady
St. Oswald's son and heir. He recently and privately married
Miss Evie Carew, whose portrait is also seen on this page

THE HON. MRS. ROWLAND WINN *E. O. Hoppé*

Née Miss Evie Carew, one of Daly's beautiful stars. She thereby
joins a large and attractive band of pilgrims who have journeyed
from the footlights to the Mecca of the peerage

Following the shocking news of Rowland and Evie's marriage, they were all over the media and in January 1916, just days after the news broke, their photographs appeared in *Tatler*.

The letter does reveal that, predictably, Lord St Oswald had been thoroughly unimpressed when he'd first heard about his son's choice of wife, and was presumably shocked if he did learn of it via the newspapers. Young Rowland, however, was desperate to persuade his father he had not erred. 'I also hope that the interview you had made you feel that it will not be so hard as you previously imagined it would be to befriend and get to know her properly.'

Depending on how Rowland perceived time, he seemed to have known Evie for at least a few months prior to the wedding, for, he said, 'I have known her so long now and think I am in a position to judge.' He reckoned she was the 'most lovable person & as refined as you could possibly wish'. But the young man was also a realist and knew he had upset his father, not least because of the way the news of the wedding had reached him.

She wrote me a letter by the next mail after going to tea at Hill Street, & couldn't say enough about it. She understands, every bit as much as I do,

how you have been hurt over it all, especially over the way the marriage
became known to you, & I am quite sure you know that we would have
given anything rather than that it should have been brought to your notice
in the sudden & unpleasant way it was!

At the time Rowland wrote this letter he was being transferred to the Royal
Flying Corps, though he would remain attached to the Coldstream Guards
until he resigned his commission in July 1919. He wrote that the 'transfer is
alright & I am due to report for duty in about a fortnight.' He also imparted
news about the war and ended his letter by wishing his father well – the man
had been in bad health with pains in his back, arms and legs.

Rowland's debts

Other letters from this period suggest that it wasn't only Rowland's love
life that had driven his father to distraction. Lord St Oswald received
a letter on 21 May 1916 from the long-standing family solicitor, G.M.
Saunders. 'I deeply sympathize,' Saunders began, 'with you and Lady
St Oswald in the great trouble your eldest son has caused you.' He went
on to say that he was pleased that Lord St Oswald had decided to 'have
no traffic with the money lenders and to let your son go bankrupt'.
For it turned out that young Rowland had been somewhat profligate
in his spending and had run out of money, despite an allowance from
his father of £700 per year. Desperate, he'd turned to Jewish money
lenders to enable him to continue his extravagant lifestyle. Bankruptcy,
Mr Saunders felt, 'is the only way of ascertaining the real extent of his
liabilities.'

In June 1916, Lord St Oswald received another letter on the matter from
his brother, George William Phipps Winn of Walton Hall, Wakefield. George
had heard from Saunders that one of the money lenders, known to him
simply as Levy, had sent a writ demanding £1,200. A hearing was due to take
place in ten days and George was sure the money lenders' demands would
be upheld. This, he wrote, would lead to the debt being officially registered,
which would then see all of Rowland's creditors send in their claims. But
any bankruptcy could not be heard in Rowland's absence (the young man
being in France with the Royal Flying Corps at the time), so 'there will be

plenty of time to negotiate with the Hebrews if this seems desirable.' George Winn had heard that Rowland had cleared out his bank account and when he was last in England he'd been borrowing even more money. It seemed bankruptcy was inevitable.

> Whatever your ultimate decision may be, I think the present proceedings should be allowed to continue & he should be given to understand that he will have to go through the Bankruptcy Court.

Later that month, Rowland, now officially with the 1st Squadron of the Royal Flying Corps, wrote to his father to thank him for paying some of his bills. One was to the tune of £100 for an 'electric canoe', which Rowland confessed to having used 'four times, I think'. This assistance allowed Rowland to present some cheques that the bank were holding and he told his 'dear pa' that he couldn't thank him enough for 'doing what you have'. He continued: 'I honestly do want to pay off any tradesmen's accounts I can if they will only wait a bit.' And he tried to assuage his father's worries by telling him that he only had 'two really large ones'.

His debts weren't mentioned when Rowland wrote again on 1 August that year to wish his father a happy birthday and to tell him he'd 'been up 3 times' in a dual control aeroplane, which he had landed 'on my lonesome'. 'The war goes on well,' he continued, 'slow but sure on this front while the Russians appear to be making great strides.'

Rowland was still in France with his squadron when he wrote again a week later. He'd been in touch with Evie (he called her Eve) who had told her husband that Lord St Oswald had offered to help pay for a property that the pair were in the process of attempting to purchase. He told his father, 'I have to-day heard from Eve to the effect that you have consented to pay the rest of our house, which she has apparently found with the help of Uncle Bunny and Mrs Leigh!' It seemed that Lord St Oswald was warming to his new daughter-in-law, if the following extract from this letter is taken at face value:

> I don't know how to thank you enough for all you have done for us and for the way in which you have taken to my Eve. I am sure you do like her.

I am writing to thank Uncle Bunny & Aunt Blanche who never seem to be able to do enough for Eve & myself.

It is such a relief when one is out here, to know that she is being well looked after.

And well might Rowland have hoped that the care of his wife was in safe hands, for she was expecting their first child. 'So if she moves into the house at once,' he wrote, 'as she says she is going to do, it will be every bit as well, as then she can get settled & everything moved in before the baby arrives!'

An update on the state of Rowland's war followed. He told his father that the enemy were 'dropping bombs round about us, in retaliation for our nightly (and daily) excursions behind [their] lines with the same purpose'. Rowland added that bombs had dropped within 400 yards of the aerodrome at which he was based, but he took it in good humour, telling his father that the bomber 'drops them and then scoots off back as fast as ever he can. It's really funny to watch!'

Bankrupt

He was probably less amused a year later when he found himself before the Windsor Bankruptcy Court, his lifestyle and money troubles finally catching up with him. A report in the *Western Times* on 3 April 1917 had this to say:

Officer in Grip of Money Lenders

Extravagant living, heavy Army expenses and large interest to moneylenders were stated to be the cause of the failure of Captain Rowland George Winn, Coldstream Guards, attached Royal Flying Corps, who appeared at the Windsor Bankruptcy Court, on Saturday, for public examination. The interest with expenses due to moneylenders was £3,828, and the personal expenditure during the past two years £2,000. His Army pay for the same period was £380, and the voluntary allowance from his father £1,400. The total liabilities amounted to £9,665 10s and the assets £34 11s 6d, leaving a deficiency of £9,630 18s 6d.

Debtor admitted that he exceeded his father's allowance of £700 a year by buying motor-cars, which, with the upkeep, proved very expensive. He also purchased a quantity of jewellery, which he gave away. In March 1915, he commenced to resort to moneylenders to meet tradesmen's bills. Considerable sums were deducted by agents through whom he was introduced to the moneylenders.

Rowland was a father by now, his son Rowland Denys Guy Winn having been born on 19 September 1916, followed, on 9 July 1919, by Derek Edward Anthony Winn.

By the time Derek was born, Rowland had lost both his parents. Lady Winn died on 14 February 1919, followed by her husband, Baron St Oswald, on 13 April 1919. Lady St Oswald died at her London residence, 19 Hill Street, Berkeley Square. The cause of her demise, double pneumonia, had struck

The new Mrs Rowland Winn with her son Rowland in 1918.

after two attacks of influenza. Death came in the midst of the flu pandemic, also known as Spanish Flu, which began in 1918 and ended in December 1920. Reporting her passing, the *Yorkshire Post and Leeds Intelligencer* wrote that 'In London society Lady St Oswald was a prominent figure, and in the neighbourhood of Nostell Priory, their Yorkshire home, her Ladyship was very popular with all classes.' A few weeks later at Torquay, Lord St Oswald succumbed to heart failure and the title was handed down to the next generation.

Less than five years into their marriage, Rowland had become the 3rd Baron St Oswald, his wife, former chorus girl Nellie Greene, was now Lady St Oswald, and an heir and a spare were secured.

And having left an estate worth £1,394,141, much of it passing to the new baron, the late Rowland Winn, through his death, had obliterated his son's money problems.

2nd Baron St Oswald, father of Rowland Winn, who became 3rd Baron St Oswald on the older man's death in 1919.

A memorial plaque to Lord and Lady St Oswald in Wragby parish church.

Evie, now Lady St Oswald, appeared in a photoshoot for *Tatler*, which was published on 5 May 1920.

LORD AND LADY ST. OSWALD

At Lord Denman's shoot at Balcombe Place, Sussex, which was a great success, and was lucky where the weather was concerned. Lord St. Oswald used to be in the Coldstream, and was wounded in the war

Lord and Lady St Oswald on a shoot at Balcombe Place, Sussex in 1922.

Epilogue

Rowland and Evie spent much of their married life away from Nostell Priory, which had been subject to the management of trustees, according to the will made by Rowland's father.

Rowland's younger siblings, Reginald, Edith and Charles (who served with the 10th Hussars, and lost an eye during the war), took up infrequent residence. Thrice-married Charles stayed most regularly; a keen pilot, he kept his own plane at Nostell, using the long drive as a runway. The house was used as a training base by the Royal Artillery Signal Training Regiment during and after the Second World War, and in July 1951 the family opened their doors to the public.

Adverts soon began appearing in the local press offering admission to the house and gardens on Wednesday and Thursday afternoons from July to October, with 'Chippendale and Period Art on show'. To access the site adults paid two shillings and sixpence and children one shilling and threepence. It was reported in October 1951 that Nostell Priory had received 10,646 visitors so far, and in April 1952, the first guidebook was published. It retailed at one shilling and threepence, one reviewer declaring that 'the historical and artistic significance is indicated with masterly brevity in the text, while the illustrations again are admirable.'

In July 1952, Rowland Winn (eldest son of the 3rd Baron St Oswald), who had come to live at Nostell at the end of the war, offered the house, grounds and lake to charity to ensure the site's long-term preservation. This offer, made with the agreement of the estate trustees, was accepted the following year and doors were reopened to the public on Easter Sunday 1954. Visitors could now attend on Wednesdays, Saturdays and Sundays from Easter to October, and any day from August to September. The family remained at the house and retained ownership of the furniture and paintings, though in the 1980s most of these were handed over to the trust that now runs the site.

The 3rd Baron died in 1957 and was succeeded by his son and namesake. The 4th Baron was a Conservative in the House of Lords, a Member of the European Parliament and also, with James Scott-Hopkins, joint Parliamentary Secretary to the Ministry of Agriculture in the early 1960s.

On 29 April 1980, a fire broke out at Nostell Priory. It tore through the Breakfast Room and caused immense damage, though work was later undertaken to restore it.

Two years before the 4th Baron's death in 1984, a music festival was held on the site. It was promoted by Theakston, a brewery based in Masham in North Yorkshire, and was held on 27 and 28 August. The band *Jethro Tull* headlined the festival, with support from *Marillion* and *Lindisfarne*, among others. Attendance was estimated at around 37,000 over the two days.

In 1984, another August Bank Holiday weekend music festival was held at Nostell, this time over four days. *The Damned, Dr and the Medics, The Band, Lindisfarne, John Kay and Steppenwolf* and *Van Morrison* were among several big names to play at the event. Tickets cost £24 for the full weekend, including free camping and parking. At the same time, a 'free' event was held in a nearby field. It descended into chaos, leading to serious disturbances. The *Daily Mail* reported that 500 police officers raided the site, to repel 'an evil drug-pushing cult'. Drugs were certainly being offered openly for sale, chalk boards describing the availability of acid, weed, cocaine and speed at low prices. Hundreds of members of a group called *Peace Convoy* who had been at the site for the past week were arrested, the newspaper reckoning some attendees of the official festival were armed with shotguns and chainsaws and were walking around naked (you'd want to be very careful rocking that particular combination). Chief Constable John Domaille, who was in charge of the raid, explained that local residents were afraid, 'and there has also been a tremendous amount of rumour.' He added that whilst no property had been damaged, 'rightly or wrongly, we decided to take this action and we waited until the public were out of the way.'

Though drugs, cash, knives, axes and spears were apparently seized, the drugs advisory charity *Release* said they doubted that so many people could have been involved in the disturbances, and that it was 'the unconventional lifestyles of the people attending the festival' that had 'led police to exceed reasonable use of their powers.' They added that mass arrests were 'no more than a fishing expedition' constituting harassment. A year later, on 1 June 1985, in an event that became known as the *Battle of the Beanfield*, police action at Stonehenge stopped *Peace Convoy* from holding the Stonehenge Free Festival, which had run since 1974. In total, 537 travellers were arrested, and this is considered to be one of the largest mass arrests in English history. A young firebrand MP who went by the name Jeremy Corbyn was reportedly outraged at the actions taken by the police.

Following the death without issue of the 4th Baron, his brother, Derek Winn, inherited the title. He oversaw the day-to-day management of the house for the trust until a couple of years before his death in 1999.

In 1991, the *Daily Express* reported that Lady St Oswald had visited Wakefield and was horrified by the litter she had found strewn about the city. She decided to return with a servant, David Halliwell, and over the next two hours she filled plastic bags with rubbish, and was at pains to understand why the locals were willing to 'put up with all the filth'. In response, a spokesman for Wakefield Council told the newspaper that Lady St Oswald was picking on them, adding, 'there are much more untidy cities than ours.'

Two years later, fed up of all her own clutter, Lady St Oswald decided to put her house in order, declaring that 'I don't think it's right that things one's not using shouldn't go to somebody else who'd be glad of them.' A fancy car boot sale was arranged and held on Nostell's grounds. Eager shoppers flocked from miles around to get their hands on the posh wares for sale. A £3,000 mink fur coat was offered for £30 and such was the demand for it, a brawl broke out, several men vying for ownership of the garment. One of those who missed out, a traveller called John Matthews, told the press that he'd placed a curse on the coat, declaring that the man who bought it would die in it. It was purchased by Peter Cottrill, a 57-year-old from Stafford who'd spent the previous night in his car, which was parked outside the priory gates, to ensure he was first through them the following day.

The house, lake and bridge shown in 1822, from J.P. Neale's *Views of the Seats, Mansions, Castles etc. of Noblemen and Gentlemen in England, Wales, Scotland and Ireland.*

He'd bought the coat for his wife, but as she was animal lover, 'who hates that sort of coat', he wondered if he'd made a mistake.

The 6th and present Baron St Oswald, who succeeded his father in 1999, is Charles Rowland Andrew Winn. He represents the Conservatives in the House of Lords, continuing a long-held family tradition in support of that political party. He is father to two children, a daughter, Henrietta, and a son, the Honourable Rowland Charles Sebastian Winn.

In 2017, an artist called Luke Jerram staged an art installation at Nostell Priory comprising 2,000 clocks and watches, all set to different times. The installation was named *Harrison's Garden* in honour of the maker of the famous 1717 wooden longcase clock that resides in the house. It was built by horologist John Harrison, who gained fame for inventing the marine chronometer to enable the calculation of longitude at sea, which greatly improved the safety of seamen on long voyages. Harrison was born in 1693 at Foulby and his father worked as a carpenter on the Nostell estate, though the family moved to Barrow upon Humber in Lincolnshire when Harrison was about six or seven. The clock at Nostell, which is still in working order, is one of three of Harrison's that survive from the period, the other two dating from 1713 and 1715, both of which are on display in London's Science Museum. Nostell's clock, inscribed 'John Harrison Barrow', was built almost twenty years before work began on the present house, and with its maker's historical associations to the family, it's perhaps fitting that it found a home within the priory.

We must leave our story here, with the clock still ticking away, and the house still proudly standing; its history not lost, but laid bare for the public to explore, and through Nostell's vast archive, to discover anew.

Appendix

An inventory of the goods of Sir Cotton Gargrave of Nostell who died in 1588. He died indebted to the Crown, having retained rents he'd collected belonging to the Duchy of Lancaster. The following transcription has been rendered into modern English.

A note of the goods of the children of Sir Cotton Gargrave valued by Leonard Reasby, John Mearinge, William Armond, gentleman, John Robinson, Henry Watkinson, Richard Clayton, 8th July 1588.

In the new great chamber
One stand bed with the teaser valance curtains of green silk, one feather bed, one bolster, one mattress, two fustian blankets, one quilt of green taffeta sarcenet, two pillows, two blankets, one Irish rug, eight green saye curtains, eleven iron rods for the curtains, one cupboard – £17
The ceiling in the chamber – £6

The next inner chamber
A standing bed, one teaser of dornix, one low bed, one feather bed, one bolster, one pair of blankets and a coverlet, three iron curtain rods and one pair of tongs – 30 shillings, 4 pence

In the gallery
The ceiling in the gallery, not praised
The maps there – 20 shillings
One press – 13 shillings, 4 pence

In the matte chamber
One bedstock, one teaser of wrought velvet, three taffeta curtains, three iron rods, one featherbed, one bolster, two pillows, one pair of blankets, one covering, a pallet, one bed, a bolster, a pair of blankets, one coverlet, one chair, one stool, one cupboard, one blue cupboard cloth, two long cushions, four hangings of Arras work – £15

In the painted chamber
A stand bed, three iron rods, five curtains, one feather bed, one bolster, one pair of blankets, one covering, two pallets, two featherbeds, two bolsters, one pair, two coverlets – £6

In the north chamber
One stand bed, one teaser and five curtains of orange tawny, one bed, one bolster, one pair of blankets, one pair of pillows, one covering, a pallet, one bed, one bolster, one pair of blankets, one coverlet, one cupboard, one cupboard cloth and one stool and five pieces of hangings of Arras work – £12

In the broken chamber
Two old hangings of Arras work – 10 shillings

In the high gallery chamber
One stand bed, one feather bed, one bolster, one pair of blankets, one pillow, two coverlets, one cupboard, one form and one old chair – 30 shillings

In the upper gallery
Two bedstocks, two featherbeds, two bolsters, two old coverings, three blankets – 40 shillings

In the nursery
Three standing beds, one trundle bed, one teaser of damask, five taffeta curtains [of] blue and yellow, one canopy, one other teaser [of] green and red cloth, five green saye curtains, three feather beds, three bolsters, three pairs of blankets, two tapestry coverings and one red covering, two cupboards, one chair, one chest and five curtain rods, and the ceiling – £15

In the inner nursery
A teaser, a stand bed and two trundle beds, three curtains of red, three feather beds, three pairs of blankets, one pillow, three reed coverings, one case of daggs [heavy pistols], two great chests, certain books – 100 shillings

In the great chamber
Two long tables, two frames, three forms [a backless bench], a dozen high buffet stools, six little buffet stools, one little square table, one cupboard, three chairs, two tablecloths and one cupboard cloth, ten cushions, seven pieces of hangings, and the ceiling – £6

In the little new chamber near to the great chamber
One framed table, two forms, two other forms joined to the ceiling – 20 shillings

In the hall
The high table, one cupboard and a form – 13 shillings and 4 pence

In the little nursery
A standing bed, one trundle bed, a teaser, four hangings, two featherbeds, two bolsters, two pairs of blankets, two coverings, two halberds [a pole weapon with an axe and spear], the ceiling – 70 shillings

The press chamber
The great press – 10 shillings
Ten pairs of linen sheets, sixteen pairs of middling sheets, twenty pairs of coarse sheets, ten pairs of harden sheets, ten pairs of pillowbears, six 'lyvie' towels, six damask napkins, six cupboard cloths, ten square cloths, six dozen napkins, six hall cloths – £16 and 9 shillings

In the kitchen
Nine brass pots and one posnet [a cooking vessel], two chafing dishes, one scummer, one brass mortar, one pestle, four spits, two cleavers, two iron ranges, two pairs of iron racks, two dripping pans, one lead, two kettles, a frying pan, pot-hooks, fire shovels – £6 13 shillings and 4 pence

In the washing house
A lead pan, three washing tubs – 13 shillings and 4 pence

In the brewhouse
One lead, three great tubs, one keeler [cooler], three soes with all other husslements – £10

In the low parlour
One table, one form, two great kettles, one pan, one posnet, two skeels [pails or tubs], ten wooden trays, six milking kits, four pewter candlesticks with other husslements – 40 shillings

In the chamber over Anthony's chamber
A bed, a bolster, one blanket and one coverlet – 20 shillings

In the armoury

Fourteen unstocked cavalier barrels, sixty-two stocked old cavaliers, two demi-lance staves [short spears], pikes and light horsemen's staves (by estimation 40), three sheafs of steal arrows with heads, three old flasks and three skulls – £14

In the second vault to the armoury

Three armours for demi-lances and three head pieces with beavers, one cuirass for a demi-lance without furniture, three corselets, one cuirass – whereof two furnished, six jacks, one mail coat, three old head pieces, certain other broken pieces of armour – £6 13 shillings and 4 pence

In the second vault on the south side of the gallery

Nine corselets with their furniture – £8 16 shillings and 8 pence
Twenty-six pikes – £46 and 8 pence

In the third vault on the north side of the gallery

Forty-five morion helmets – £4 and 10 shillings
Two burgonet helmets and diverse other parcels of armour – 10 shillings

In the house [In an earlier transcription of this material from a Yorkshire Archaeological Journal, volume 11, published in 1891, the transcriber, J.J. Cartwright, suggested that the items that follow were held at the Gargraves' manor house in Upton. However, this is not made clear in the original source material.]

All the goods in the house with certain walnut tree timber – 40 shillings
Two bound wains and one unbound, three ploughs, eight yokes, seven iron teams, seven stand hecks, with all furniture thereto belonging – £7
Twelve oxen – £46
Three kine – 100 shillings
Ten score and twelve sheep – £46
Barley on the ground (33 acres) – £30
Peas and oats (42 acres) – £13 six shillings and 8 pence
Forty sheep bars – 20 shillings
Ten swine – 100 shillings
In Halleley closes, twenty-four steers – £213 6 shillings and 8 pence
In the Windmill field, twenty-four steers – £133 6 shillings and 8 pence
Twenty-three kine – £44
Two more kine, seven heifers, one stirk, three elder cows, four bullocks – £20

Twenty-two acres of barley – £26 13 shillings and 4 pence
Thirty acres of wheat at Horncastle Hill – £45
Forty acres of oats at Swalerodes – £26 13 shillings and 4 pence
Twenty draught Nostell oxen – £24
Sixty Kinsley Park fat wethers – £25
Lambs and other sheep put to feed – £73 and 4 pence

In the great chamber there [Cartwright assumed this was another reference to the house at Upton. Certainly the appraisal that follows appears to describe goods held away from Nostell given the description of rooms such as the 'great chamber', which had already been appraised at Nostell.]
A new bedstead, four featherbeds, four bolsters, four pillows, one pair of fustian blankets [heavy woven cloth], two pairs of woollen blankets, three taffeta curtains, one yellow teaser, five curtains, one red and green teaser, five curtains, and three green curtains – £20
A long Turkey carpet cloth, one cupboard cloth, one new long tapestry cushion, two other tapestries, cupboard cloths, two Turkey cupboard cloths, four silk cushions, two little cushions, one chair, one cupboard and one stool – £12
A pair of virginals – 40 shillings

In the next chamber to the great chamber
A cupboard and three pieces of hangings of Arras work – £12

In the wardrobe
A great chest and two presses – £26 and 8 pence
In the 'Mr' Chamber three pairs of fine linen sheets, three pairs of pillowbears, two pairs of coarse sheets of three breadths, six pairs of linen sheets of two breadths, and one iron bound chest – £12 six shillings and 8 pence
A long tablecloth, a cupboard cloth and one towel of imagery – 40 shillings
A tablecloth, one towel, one cupboard cloth of damask of flowers – 40 shillings
Four tablecloths of damask work and diaper, two cupboard cloths and two towels – £6 13 shillings and 4 pence
A tablecloth, one cupboard cloth, one towel of diaper – 40 shillings
Two arming towels of diaper – 5 shillings
Fourteen diaper and damask napkins – 30 shillings
Four long tablecloths, four long towels, four dozen napkins, three cupboard cloths, three short towels – £4 and 10 shillings
A Flanders chest and one field bed – 20 shillings

In the inner chamber
Two low bedsteads, one cupboard, and one chest – 20 shillings

In the dining parlour
A long table with a frame, a square table, one cupboard, one form, six high stools, four little stools, and nine without covers, two green tablecloths, and one cupboard cloth – 30 shillings

Pewter vessels
One dozen weighing 42lb, one other dozen weighing 30lb, one other weighing 44lb, and one other weighing 16lb, one other weighing 12lb, one other weighing 8lb, twenty platters weighing 15lb, one other dozen weighing 12lb, two other platters weighing 5lb, and two chargers weighing 14lb, in all – £4 6 shillings and 10 pence

Plates, pottingers and saucers – 7 shillings

Six candlesticks – 4 shillings

Four chamber pots – 3 shillings and 4 pence

Five basins and two ewers and one odd dish – 14 shillings

Two pewter pots – 10 shillings

In the kitchen
One iron range, one pair of racks, three gallipots, seven spits, one beef lead – 53 shillings and 4 pence

Two brass mortars, one pestle, two brass pots, one posnet, three brass pans, two skillets with covers, one frying pan, two dripping pans, one gird iron [griddle iron], one shredding knife, two chopping knives, one copper oven, and the shelves – £5

In the brewhouse
The lead with all the brewing vessels there – £4

The goods in the backhouse & bolting house – 40 shillings

[Back at] Nostell

In the kitchen
Seven new dishes, seven platters, seven little saucers, seven little dishes weighing 65lbs – 30 shillings

Sixteen old dishes, eight old platters, two great chargers weighing 55lbs – 22 shillings, 10 pence

In the buttery
Two pewter pots, two basins, two ewers, a white candlestick, red candlesticks, two pewter salts, one voider, three little pewter pots, three hand basins, and three chamber pots – 30 shillings

Horses
One stoned colt – £6
One white-grey mare – £5
One Black gelding – £5
Grey Pit – 53 shillings, 4 pence
Six work horses – £8
Two milne [dialect word for mill] horses – 53 shillings, 4 pence
Two little nags – 60 shillings
One grey gelding – £6
One little colt foal – 20 shillings

Nostell
Four iron bound wains, three bare wains furnishes – £5
Sixteen yokes furnished with irons and four pairs of iron teams – 25 shillings
Eleven more iron teams – 20 shillings
Two oxen harrows with iron teeth – 10 shillings
Six pairs of horse harrows furnished – 24 shillings
Ten stave hecks – 26 shillings
One iron bound cart – 5 shillings
One brewing lead in the lathe yard – 12 shillings

Swine
Of the greatest sort, twenty – £8
Of the lesser sort, twelve – 48 shillings
Pigs, twenty-six – 52 shillings

Corn at Nostell and Kinsley
Wheat threshed and unthreshed, thirty quarters – £24
Malt, 120 quarters – £72
Peas, fifteen quarters – £7

Wool
Forty stones of wool – £10

In the old nursery
A bed, a bolster, a pair of blankets, one cupboard and a range – 33 shillings, 4 pence

In the cloak chamber
A bed, a mattress, one bolster, two coverlets – 13 shillings, 4 pence

In Anthony's chamber
A bed, a bolster, a pair of blankets, and two coverlets – 40 shillings

Plate
White plate at 4 shillings, 6 pence per oz 726 oz – £163, 7 shillings
Parcel gilt at 4 shillings, 8 pence per oz 103 oz – £24, 8 pence
Gilt plate at 6 shillings per oz 304 oz – £91, 4 shillings
£282, 18 shillings, 4 pence

Total £1,189, 5 shillings, 8 pence

Leonarde Reasbie
Willm Hawmonde
John Mearinge
Henrie Watkinson
Richard Clayton
John Robinson

Additions upon my Lady's confession of goods omitted in this inventory
A chain of gold estimated at £40
Two coach horses, the coach and a litter [a vehicle without wheels in which
    passengers sat whilst carried by servants] £20
Certain books estimated at 100 shillings
Debt by obligations due by Mr Wentworth and paid at the death of Sir Cotton – £600
The tithe corn at Fryston over besides the rent reserved – £30

Sum total – £695
Total – £2,214, 5 shillings, 8 pence

Memorandum that one Francis Corker stand indebted upon a mortgage for land in
    the sum of – £400
Also that one Ambrose Halleley stand indebted for a mortgage for term of years of
    certain called Halliley closes in the sum of – £100

A Note on Sources

In writing the stories for this book a large number of sources were consulted. Whilst I haven't included specific references to illustrate each and every single one – far too tedious an endeavour for both reader and writer alike – I will briefly discuss a selection of the main sources.

The principal primary source material can be found in the Nostell Priory and Winn family archive, which is housed at the new West Yorkshire History Centre, situated on Lower Kirkgate in Wakefield. The catalogue finding number for this huge collection of material is WYW1352. It comprises, among other things, personal papers, estate papers, plans, deeds and many letters. In 2013, a project to catalogue the collection was launched. It was funded by The National Archives and saw a vastly improved catalogue placed online at www.catalogue.wyjs.org.uk, where individual items within the collection can be browsed, and the various documents cited within this book easily identified.

Other primary sources can be found at The National Archives in Kew. These include a list of the allegations levelled against the prior and his canons at St Oswald's during the dissolution, and are located within series SP1, part of the State Papers of Henry VIII. Additionally, the registered wills of Thomas Legh and Dame Sabine Louise Winn, among other wills I have cited, form part of the Prerogative Court Canterbury collection, appearing in series PROB 11. The wills in this series can be viewed online at www.nationalarchives.gov.uk or www.ancestry.co.uk, subject to crossing the relevant palms with the appropriate amounts of silver, or you could just visit Kew and see them for free.

Also at Kew are the Court of King's Bench indictments against Thomas Gargrave. These are held within series KB 9 and as there is no index, they take a bit of finding.

The Duchy of Lancaster: Special Commissions and Returns series, found at DL 44, contains the documents, including the inventory cited in the appendix, relating to the commission set up to seize property belonging to Sir Cotton Gargrave, following his death. A inquisition post-mortem was carried out when Sir Cotton died, which confirmed that his real estate at Nostell was entailed and was to be inherited by his son, Thomas. This inquisition is held in series C 142, which comprises Chancery Inquisitions.

A transcription of most of the will of Sir Thomas Gargrave, father of Sir Cotton, appears in J.J. Cartwright's *Chapters in the History of Yorkshire*, published in 1872. A copy of the will is kept in the British Library Additional Manuscript series, at reference 24475.

The wills of James Pilkington, Bishop of Durham, Sir Cotton Gargrave and Sir Rowland Winn, 4th Baronet, can be found in collections held at the Borthwick Institute at the University of York, whose *Borthwick Papers* series includes (as paper number 111) *The Foundation of Nostell Priory* by Judith A. Frost. Dr Frost's 2005 PhD thesis on the same topic is entitled *An Edition of the Nostell Priory Cartulary*, and contains translations of documents relating to Nostell's earliest recorded history. The University of York hold a copy.

Elizabethan period letters referring to the Rising of the North and Thomas Gargrave's behaviour towards his stepmother are part of the *Talbot Papers*, found at MS 3196, 3198 and 3200. These can be read at Lambeth Palace Library. Many of the letters to and from Sir Thomas Gargrave written during the time of the Rising of the North were published in *Memorials of the Rebellion in 1569*, edited by Sir Cuthbert Sharp and published in 1840.

The Galway Collection at Nottingham University, in series Ga 9948, contains the lease that formed part of the marriage settlement upon the wedding of Thomas Gargrave and Catherine Wentworth.

The Wentworth Woodhouse papers at Sheffield City Archives in series WWM/Str include Sir William Wentworth's handbook of advice for his son, Thomas Wentworth, which is dated 1604.

Other useful sources include a project called *The Charters of William II and Henry I* run by Professor Richard Sharpe and David X. Carpenter of the University of Oxford. This can be browsed at https://actswilliam2henry1.wordpress.com.

There is also Northern Archaeological Associates' 2001 report entitled *Nostell Priory, West Yorkshire Archaeological Property Survey*, and T.G. Wright's unpublished manuscript *Reminiscences of Nostell* (Wright was the Winn family doctor). Both of these are held by the Yorkshire Archaeological and Historical Society, and both are to be found in the Special Collections at Leeds University Library.

Articles quoted from newspapers are mainly held within the British Library's British Newspaper Archive, which can be browsed at www.britishnewspaperarchive.co.uk.

Parish registers containing notices of Gargrave and Winn family baptisms, marriages and burials are held at the West Yorkshire Archive Service, Wakefield; Manchester Archives and Local Studies; Cheshire Archives and Local Studies; Lincolnshire Archives; and London Metropolitan Archives.

As for books, I have made regular reference to the second volume of Reverend Joseph Hunter's epic *South Yorkshire: the History and Topography of the Deanery of Doncaster*, which he published in 1831, following the first volume's publication in 1828. Hunter arranged these books on a parish by parish basis, the antiquities and topographies of each parish and their constituent townships described in fine detail. Among all the parochial descriptions is a standalone chapter entitled *The Priory of St Oswald of Nostel* in which Hunter presented his version of Nostell's history from its foundation to the tenure of Charles Winn, who was living at Nostell during Hunter's lifetime. Although some of what Hunter wrote about Nostell is flawed, his consultation of (some now lost) original sources makes his *South Yorkshire* a vital resource for any student of Nostell Priory. Hunter draws on John Burton's 1758 *Monasticon Eboracense*, which includes a list of the endowments that St Oswald's received.

Letters cited from the time of the dissolution appear in James Gardiner's *Letters and Papers of Henry VIII*, volumes XII and XIII, published in 1890 and 1892. Another account of the ecclesiastical history of St Oswald's Priory can be found in *A History of the County of York*: volume III, edited by William Page and published as part of the Victoria County History series in 1974. There is also *An Historical Sketch of the The Priory of St Oswald at Nostel* by R.E. Batty, vicar of Wragby, which was published by the Yorkshire Architectural Society in 1858. And if you want to try a scholarly tome about monasticism in Yorkshire, with copious references to Nostell, then a particularly good one is Janet Burton's *The Monastic Order in Yorkshire 1069–1215*, published in 1999 by Cambridge University Press.

Topographers John Leland of the Tudor period, Roger Dodsworth of the seventeenth century and Thomas Frognall Dibdin, writing at the birth of the Victorian era, all provide interesting descriptions of Nostell and Wragby church. Leland's work was published in several volumes from 1907 to 1910, edited by Lucy Toulmin-Smith. It was titled *The Itinerary of John Leland in our about the years 1535–1543*. Dodsworth's visit to Wragby parish church was included in *Dodsworth's Church Notes, 1619–1631*, published by the Yorkshire Archaeological and Historical Society in volume thirty-four of their Record Series, and Dibdin's adventures were published in 1838 as *A Biographical, Antiquarian and Picturesque Tour in the Northern Counties and in Scotland*.

Cardinal Wolsey's visit to Nostell in 1530, recorded contemporaneously by his gentleman-usher, George Cavendish, formed part of his biography about Wolsey. Samuel Singer's edition of Cavendish's biography appeared in 1825 as *The Life of Cardinal Wolsey*.

A transcription of the conveyance of Nostell to the Gargraves can be found in *Feet of Fines of the Tudor Period*, which makes up volume two of the Yorkshire Archaeological and Historical Society's Record Series, published in 1887.

And on the subject of the Gargraves, accounts of Sir Thomas and Sir Cotton Gargrave, specifically concerning their careers in Parliament, appear in *The History of Parliament: the House of Commons: 1558–1603*, edited by P.W. Hasler and published in 1981.

A very good general history of Yorkshire including a brief description of the building of the present Nostell Priory can be found in David Hey's *A History of Yorkshire*, published in 2005. Catherine Cappe's *Memoirs*, published in 1822, contain an account of her time at Nostell during the 1760s, which is lively, if a little one-sided.

A History of Ackworth School, published in 1853, discussed the Winns' involvement with the foundling hospital, which was formerly in operation on the same site.

A fine biography of Thomas Chippendale appears in the 1978 book *The Life and Work of Thomas Chippendale* by Christopher Gilbert, in which the author does a good job of demolishing the idea that Chippendale constructed the Nostell dolls' house.

Christopher Todd's 2005 paper *A Swiss Milady in Yorkshire: Sabine Winn of Nostell Priory* is in volume seventy-seven of the *Yorkshire Archaeological Journal*.

Biographical details of the various University of Cambridge students described in these stories come from *Alumni Cantabrigienses*, by John Venn senior and John Venn junior, published in ten volumes from 1922 to 1954 by Cambridge University Press.

Art historian Maurice Walter Brockwell published, in a limited run of 300 copies, a catalogue of the paintings housed at Nostell Priory, which was called *The Nostell Collection*, printed in 1915. Among the gems within this scarce book is an interesting history of Nostell, alongside short biographies of the baronets and barons. Brockwell made use of many original sources in the Nostell archive when compiling these.

The best short guide book about Nostell is titled *Nostell Priory and Parkland*. It was written by Sophie Raikes and Tim Knox and published in 2008.

And lastly, interesting information about the music festivals held at Nostell Priory in the 1980s can be found at the UK Rock Festivals website at www.ukrockfestivals.co.uk.

Index